Scottish
Metrical
Psalter

Scottish Metrical Psalter

PSALMS OF DAVID IN METRE

EREMITICAL PRESS

POINT ROBERTS, WASHINGTON

Scottish Metrical Psalter: Psalms of David in Metre

Library of Congress Control Number 2007907987
ISBN-10 0-9800817-0-X
ISBN-13 978-0-9800817-0-1
This edition © 2007 Eremitical Press
Cover photo by Ove Tøpfer

Manufactured in the United States of America or the United Kingdom as
indicated on final page

10   9   8   7   6   5   4   3   2   1

In Memoriam
Iain Donald Cameron

"I to the hills will lift mine eyes
from whence doth come mine aid."
—*Psalm 121 verse 1*

PREFACE

The Scottish Metrical Psalter of 1650 was the result of many years' labor and many cycles of revisions. At least ten earlier translations were consulted to produce the version you now have in your hands. The results were so successful that for several centuries the Church of Scotland would use only these psalms and some other scriptural paraphrases for its English-language hymns. Each psalm is rendered in a regular metre that can be sung to any melody that follows that rhythm. For example, the indication *8,6,8,6* or Common Metre (C.M.) at the head of a text indicates that the first and third lines of each stanza have eight syllables, while the second and fourth have six. The greatest legacy of the Scottish Metrical Psalter is its translation of Psalm 23, which many can quote by heart, though few realize that the words come from the Scottish Metrical Psalter: "The Lord's my Shepherd, I'll not want: / He maketh me down to lie / In pastures green; he leadeth me / The quiet waters by." It is with great pleasure that Eremitical Press makes this new edition available to the reading public.

Psalm 1

8,6,8,6

[1]That man hath perfect blessedness,
   who walketh not astray
In counsel of ungodly men,
   nor stands in sinners' way,

Nor sitteth in the scorner's chair:
   [2]But placeth his delight
Upon God's law, and meditates
   on his law day and night.

[3]He shall be like a tree that grows
   near planted by a river,
Which in his season yields his fruit,
   and his leaf fadeth never:

And all he doth shall prosper well.
   [4]The wicked are not so;
But like they are unto the chaff,
   which wind drives to and fro.

[5]In judgment therefore shall not stand
   such as ungodly are;
Nor in th' assembly of the just
   shall wicked men appear.

[6]For why? the way of godly men
   unto the Lord is known:
Whereas the way of wicked men
   shall quite be overthrown.

Psalm 2

8,6,8,6

¹Why rage the heathen? and vain things
    why do the people mind?
²Kings of the earth do set themselves,
    and princes are combined,

To plot against the Lord, and his
    Anointed, saying thus,
³Let us asunder break their bands,
    and cast their cords from us.

⁴He that in heaven sits shall laugh;
    the Lord shall scorn them all.
⁵Then shall he speak to them in wrath,
    in rage he vex them shall.

⁶Yet, notwithstanding, I have him
    to be my King appointed;
And over Zion, my holy hill,
    I have him King anointed.

⁷The sure decree I will declare:
    The Lord hath said to me,
Thou art mine only Son; this day
    I have begotten thee.

⁸Ask of me, and for heritage
    the heathen I'll make thine;
And, for possession, I to thee
    will give earth's utmost line.

⁹Thou shalt, as with a weighty rod
    of iron, break them all;
And, as a potter's sherd, thou shalt
    them dash in pieces small.

¹⁰Now therefore, kings, be wise; be taught,
    ye judges of the earth:
¹¹Serve God in fear, and see that ye
    join trembling with your mirth.

¹²Kiss ye the Son, lest in his ire
   ye perish from the way,
If once his wrath begin to burn:
   blessed all that on him stay.

Psalm 3

A Psalm of David, when he fled from Absalom his son.

8,6,8,6

¹O Lord, how are my foes increased?
   against me many rise.
²Many say of my soul, For him
   in God no succour lies.

³Yet thou my shield and glory art,
   th' uplifter of mine head.
⁴I cried, and, from his holy hill,
   the Lord me answer made.

⁵I laid me down and slept; I waked;
   for God sustained me.
⁶I will not fear though thousands ten
   set round against me be.

⁷Arise, O Lord; save me, my God;
   for thou my foes hast stroke
All on the cheek-bone, and the teeth
   of wicked men hast broke.

⁸Salvation doth appertain
   unto the Lord alone:
Thy blessing, Lord, for evermore
   thy people is upon.

Psalm 4

To the chief Musician on Neginoth, A Psalm of David.

8,6,8,6

¹Give ear unto me when I call,
   God of my righteousness:
Have mercy, hear my pray'r; thou hast
   enlarged me in distress.

²O ye the sons of men! how long
   will ye love vanities?

How long my glory turn to shame,
   and will ye follow lies?

[3]But know, that for himself the Lord
   the godly man doth choose:
The Lord, when I on him do call,
   to hear will not refuse.

[4]Fear, and sin not; talk with your heart
   on bed, and silent be.
[5]Off'rings present of righteousness,
   and in the Lord trust ye.

[6]O who will show us any good?
   is that which many say:
But of thy countenance the light,
   Lord, lift on us alway.

[7]Upon my heart, bestowed by thee,
   more gladness I have found
Than they, ev'n then, when corn and wine
   did most with them abound.

[8]I will both lay me down in peace,
   and quiet sleep will take;
Because thou only me to dwell
   in safety, Lord, dost make.

Psalm 5

To the chief Musician, upon Nehiloth, A Psalm of David.

8,6,8,6

[1]Give ear unto my words, O Lord,
   my meditation weigh.
[2]Hear my loud cry, my King, my God;
   for I to thee will pray.

[3]Lord, thou shalt early hear my voice:
   I early will direct
My pray'r to thee; and, looking up,
   an answer will expect.

⁴For thou art not a God that doth
　　in wickedness delight;
Neither shall evil dwell with thee,
　　⁵Nor fools stand in thy sight.

All that ill-doers are thou hat'st;
　　⁶Cutt'st off that liars be:
The bloody and deceitful man
　　abhorred is by thee.

⁷But I into thy house will come
　　in thine abundant grace;
And I will worship in thy fear
　　toward thy holy place.

⁸Because of those mine enemies,
　　Lord, in thy righteousness
Do thou me lead; do thou thy way
　　make straight before my face.

⁹For in their mouth there is no truth,
　　their inward part is ill;
Their throat's an open sepulchre,
　　their tongue doth flatter still.

¹⁰O God, destroy them; let them be
　　by their own counsel quelled:
Them for their many sins cast out,
　　for they 'gainst thee rebelled.

¹¹But let all joy that trust in thee,
　　and still make shouting noise;
For them thou sav'st; let all that love
　　thy name in thee rejoice.

¹²For, Lord, unto the righteous man
　　thou wilt thy blessing yield:
With favour thou wilt compass him
　　about, as with a shield.

Psalm 6

To the chief Musician on Neginoth upon Sheminith, A
Psalm of David.

First Version (L.M.)
8,8,8,8

¹Lord, in thy wrath rebuke me not;
Nor in thy hot rage chasten me.
²Lord, pity me, for I am weak:
    Heal me, for my bones vexed be.

³My soul is also vexed sore;
But, Lord, how long stay wilt thou make?
⁴Return, O Lord, my soul set free;
    O save me, for thy mercies' sake.

⁵Because those that deceased are
Of thee shall no remembrance have;
And who is he that will to thee
    Give praises lying in the grave?

⁶I with my groaning weary am,
I also all the night my bed
Have caused for to swim; and I
    With tears my couch have watered.

⁷Mine eye, consumed with grief, grows old,
Because of all mine enemies.
⁸Hence from me, wicked workers all;
    For God hath heard my weeping cries.

⁹God hath my supplication heard,
My pray'r received graciously
¹⁰Shamed and sore vex'd be all my foes,
Shamed and back turned suddenly.

Psalm 6

Second Version (C.M.)
8,6,8,6

¹In thy great indignation,
    O Lord, rebuke me not;
Nor on me lay thy chast'ning hand,
    in thy displeasure hot.

2Lord, I am weak, therefore on me
   have mercy, and me spare:
Heal me, O Lord, because thou know'st
   my bones much vexed are.

3My soul is vexed sore: but, Lord,
   how long stay wilt thou make?
4Return, Lord, free my soul; and save
   me, for thy mercies' sake.

5Because of thee in death there shall
   no more remembrance be:
Of those that in the grave do lie,
   who shall give thanks to thee?

6I with my groaning weary am,
   and all the night my bed
I caused for to swim; with tears
   my couch I watered.

7By reason of my vexing grief,
   mine eye consumed is;
It waxeth old, because of all
   that be mine enemies.

8But now, depart from me all ye
   that work iniquity:
For why? the Lord hath heard my voice,
   when I did mourn and cry.

9Unto my supplication
   the Lord did hearing give:
When I to him my prayer make,
   the Lord will it receive.

10Let all be shamed and troubled sore,
   That en'mies are to me;
Let them turn back, and suddenly
   ashamed let them be.

Psalm 7

*Shiggaion of David, which he sang unto the Lord,
concerning the words of Cush the Benjamite.*

8,6,8,6

¹O Lord my God, in thee do I
   my confidence repose:
Save and deliver me from all
   my persecuting foes;

²Lest that the enemy my soul
   should, like a lion, tear,
In pieces rending it, while there
   is no deliverer.

³O Lord my God, if it be so
   that I committed this;
If it be so that in my hands
   iniquity there is:

⁴If I rewarded ill to him
   that was at peace with me;
(Yea, ev'n the man that without cause
   my foe was I did free;)

⁵Then let the foe pursue and take
   my soul, and my life thrust
Down to the earth, and let him lay
   mine honour in the dust.

⁶Rise in thy wrath, Lord, raise thyself,
   for my foes raging be;
And, to the judgment which thou hast
   commanded, wake for me.

⁷So shall th' assembly of thy folk
   about encompass thee:
Thou, therefore, for their sakes, return
   unto thy place on high.

⁸The Lord he shall the people judge:
   my judge, Jehovah, be,
After my righteousness, and mine
   integrity in me.

[9]O let the wicked's malice end;
 but stablish stedfastly
The righteous: for the righteous God
 the hearts and reins doth try.

[10]In God, who saves th' upright in heart,
 is my defence and stay.
[11]God just men judgeth, God is wroth
 with ill men ev'ry day.

[12]If he do not return again,
 then he his sword will whet;
His bow he hath already bent,
 and hath it ready set:

[13]He also hath for him prepared
 the instruments of death;
Against the persecutors he
 his shafts ordained hath.

[14]Behold, he with iniquity
 doth travail, as in birth;
A mischief he conceived hath,
 and falsehood shall bring forth.

[15]He made a pit and digged it deep,
 another there to take;
But he is fall'n into the ditch
 which he himself did make.

[16]Upon his own head his mischief
 shall be returned home;
His vi'lent dealing also down
 on his own pate shall come.

[17]According to his righteousness
 the Lord I'll magnify;
And will sing praise unto the name
 of God that is most high.

Psalm 8

To the chief Musician upon Gittith, A Psalm of David.

8,6,8,6

[1]How excellent in all the earth,
    Lord, our Lord, is thy name!
Who hast thy glory far advanced
    above the starry frame.

[2]From infants' and from sucklings' mouth
    thou didest strength ordain,
For thy foes' cause, that so thou might'st
    th' avenging foe restrain.

[3]When I look up unto the heav'ns,
    which thine own fingers framed,
Unto the moon, and to the stars,
    which were by thee ordained;

[4]Then say I, What is man, that he
    remembered is by thee?
Or what the son of man, that thou
    so kind to him should'st be?

[5]For thou a little lower hast
    him than the angels made;
With glory and with dignity
    thou crowned hast his head.

[6]Of thy hands' works thou mad'st him lord,
    all under's feet didst lay;
[7]All sheep and oxen, yea, and beasts
    that in the field do stray;

[8]Fowls of the air, fish of the sea,
    all that pass through the same.
[9]How excellent in all the earth,
    Lord, our Lord, is thy name!

Psalm 9

To the chief Musician upon Muth-labben, A Psalm of David.

8,6,8,6

[1]Lord, thee I'll praise with all my heart,
 thy wonders all proclaim.
[2]In thee, most High, I'll greatly joy,
 and sing unto thy name.

[3]When back my foes were turned, they fell,
 and perished at thy sight:
[4]For thou maintain'dst my right and cause;
 on throne sat'st judging right.

[5]The heathen thou rebuked hast,
 the wicked overthrown;
Thou hast put out their names, that they
 may never more be known.

[6]O en'my! now destructions have
 an end perpetual:
Thou cities razed; perished with them
 is their memorial.

[7]God shall endure for aye; he doth
 for judgment set his throne;
[8]In righteousness to judge the world,
 justice to give each one.

[9]God also will a refuge be
 for those that are oppressed;
A refuge will he be in times
 of trouble to distressed.

[10]And they that know thy name, in thee
 their confidence will place:
For thou hast not forsaken them
 that truly seek thy face.

[11]O sing ye praises to the Lord,
 that dwells in Zion hill;
And all the nations among
 his deeds record ye still.

[12]When he enquireth after blood,
    he then rememb'reth them:
The humble folk he not forgets
    that call upon his name.

[13]Lord, pity me; behold the grief
    which I from foes sustain;
Ev'n thou, who from the gates of death
    dost raise me up again;

[14]That I, in Zion's daughters' gates,
    may all thy praise advance;
And that I may rejoice always
    in thy deliverance.

[15]The heathen are sunk in the pit
    which they themselves prepared;
And in the net which they have hid
    their own feet fast are snared.

[16]The Lord is by the judgment known
    which he himself hath wrought:
The sinners' hands do make the snares
    wherewith themselves are caught.

[17]They who are wicked into hell
    each one shall turned be;
And all the nations that forget
    to seek the Lord most high.

[18]For they that needy are shall not
    forgotten be alway;
The expectation of the poor
    shall not be lost for aye.

[19]Arise, Lord, let not man prevail;
    judge heathen in thy sight:
[20]That they may know themselves but men,
    the nations, Lord, affright.

Psalm 10

8,6,8,6

¹Wherefore is it that thou, O Lord,
    dost stand from us afar?
And wherefore hidest thou thyself,
    when times so troublous are?

²The wicked in his loftiness
    doth persecute the poor:
In these devices they have framed
    let them be taken sure.

³The wicked of his heart's desire
    doth talk with boasting great;
He blesseth him that's covetous,
    whom yet the Lord doth hate.

⁴The wicked, through his pride of face,
    on God he doth not call;
And in the counsels of his heart
    the Lord is not at all.

⁵His ways they always grievous are;
    thy judgments from his sight
Removed are: at all his foes
    he puffeth with despight.

⁶Within his heart he thus hath said,
    I shall not moved be;
And no adversity at all
    shall ever come to me.

⁷His mouth with cursing, fraud, deceit,
    is filled abundantly;
And underneath his tongue there is
    mischief and vanity.

⁸He closely sits in villages;
    he slays the innocent:
Against the poor that pass him by
    his cruel eyes are bent.

⁹He, lion-like, lurks in his den;
    he waits the poor to take;

And when he draws him in his net,
   his prey he doth him make.

[10]Himself he humbleth very low,
   he croucheth down withal,
That so a multitude of poor
   may by his strong ones fall.

[11]He thus hath said within his heart,
   The Lord hath quite forgot;
He hides his countenance, and he
   for ever sees it not.

[12]O Lord, do thou arise; O God,
   lift up thine hand on high:
Put not the meek afflicted ones
   out of thy memory.

[13]Why is it that the wicked man
   thus doth the Lord despise?
Because that God will it require
   he in his heart denies.

[14]Thou hast it seen; for their mischief
   and spite thou wilt repay:
The poor commits himself to thee;
   thou art the orphan's stay.

[15]The arm break of the wicked man,
   and of the evil one;
Do thou seek out his wickedness,
   until thou findest none.

[16]The Lord is King through ages all,
   ev'n to eternity;
The heathen people from his land
   are perished utterly.

[17]O Lord, of those that humble are
   thou the desire didst hear;
Thou wilt prepare their heart, and thou
   to hear wilt bend thine ear;

¹⁸To judge the fatherless, and those
    that are oppressed sore;
That man, that is but sprung of earth,
    may them oppress no more.

Psalm 11

To the chief Musician, A Psalm of David.

                                       8,6,8,6

¹I in the Lord do put my trust:
    how is it then that ye
Say to my soul, Flee, as a bird,
    unto your mountain high?

²For, lo, the wicked bend their bow,
    their shafts on string they fit,
That those who upright are in heart
    they privily may hit.

³If the foundations be destroyed,
    what hath the righteous done?
⁴God in his holy temple is,
    in heaven is his throne:

His eyes do see, his eye-lids try
    ⁵men's sons. The just he proves:
But his soul hates the wicked man,
    and him that vi'lence loves.

⁶Snares, fire and brimstone, furious storms,
    on sinners he shall rain:
This, as the portion of their cup,
    doth unto them pertain.

⁷Because the Lord most righteous doth
    in righteousness delight;
And with a pleasant countenance
    beholdeth the upright.

Psalm 12

To the chief Musician upon Sheminith, A Psalm of David.

8,6,8,6

¹Help, Lord, because the godly man
    doth daily fade away;
And from among the sons of men
    the faithful do decay.

²Unto his neighbour ev'ry one
    doth utter vanity:
They with a double heart do speak,
    and lips of flattery.

³God shall cut off all flatt'ring lips,
    tongues that speak proudly thus,
⁴We'll with our tongue prevail, our lips
    are ours: who's lord o'er us?

⁵For poor oppressed, and for the sighs
    of needy, rise will I,
Saith God, and him in safety set
    from such as him defy.

⁶The words of God are words most pure;
    they be like silver tried
In earthen furnace, seven times
    that hath been purified.

⁷Lord, thou shalt them preserve and keep
    for ever from this race.
⁸On each side walk the wicked, when
    vile men are high in place.

Psalm 13

To the chief Musician, A Psalm of David.

8,6,8,6

¹How long wilt thou forget me, Lord?
  shall it for ever be?
O how long shall it be that thou
  wilt hide thy face from me?

²How long take counsel in my soul,
  still sad in heart, shall I?
How long exalted over me
  shall be mine enemy?

³O Lord my God, consider well,
  and answer to me make:
Mine eyes enlighten, lest the sleep
  of death me overtake:

⁴Lest that mine enemy should say,
  Against him I prevailed;
And those that trouble me rejoice,
  when I am moved and failed.

⁵But I have all my confidence
  thy mercy set upon;
My heart within me shall rejoice
  in thy salvation.

⁶I will unto the Lord my God
  sing praises cheerfully,
Because he hath his bounty shown
  to me abundantly.

Psalm 14

To the chief Musician, A Psalm of David.

8,6,8,6

¹That there is not a God, the fool
  doth in his heart conclude:
They are corrupt, their works are vile;
  not one of them doth good.

²Upon men's sons the Lord from heav'n
  did cast his eyes abroad,

To see if any understood,
and did seek after God.

³They altogether filthy are,
they all aside are gone;
And there is none that doeth good,
yea, sure there is not one.

⁴These workers of iniquity
do they not know at all,
That they my people eat as bread,
and on God do not call?

⁵There feared they much; for God is with
the whole race of the just.
⁶You shame the counsel of the poor,
because God is his trust.

⁷Let Isr'el's help from Zion come:
when back the Lord shall bring
His captives, Jacob shall rejoice,
and Israel shall sing.

Psalm 15

A Psalm of David.

8,6,8,6

¹Within thy tabernacle, Lord,
who shall abide with thee?
And in thy high and holy hill
who shall a dweller be?

²The man that walketh uprightly,
and worketh righteousness,
And as he thinketh in his heart,
so doth he truth express.

³Who doth not slander with his tongue,
nor to his friend doth hurt;
Nor yet against his neighbour doth
take up an ill report.

⁴In whose eyes vile men are despised;
but those that God do fear

He honoureth; and changeth not,
    though to his hurt he swear.

[5]His coin puts not to usury,
    nor take reward will he
Against the guiltless. Who doth thus
    shall never moved be.

Psalm 16

Michtam of David.

8,6,8,6

[1]Lord, keep me; for I trust in thee.
    [2]To God thus was my speech,
Thou art my Lord; and unto thee
    my goodness doth not reach:

[3]To saints on earth, to th' excellent,
    where my delight's all placed.
[4]Their sorrows shall be multiplied
    to other gods that haste:

Of their drink-offerings of blood
    I will no off'ring make;
Yea, neither I their very names
    up in my lips will take.

[5]God is of mine inheritance
    and cup the portion;
The lot that fallen is to me
    thou dost maintain alone.

[6]Unto me happily the lines
    in pleasant places fell;
Yea, the inheritance I got
    in beauty doth excel.

[7]I bless the Lord, because he doth
    by counsel me conduct;
And in the seasons of the night
    my reins do me instruct.

[8]Before me still the Lord I set:
    sith it is so that he

Doth ever stand at my right hand,
    I shall not moved be.

9Because of this my heart is glad,
    and joy shall be expressed
Ev'n by my glory; and my flesh
    in confidence shall rest.

10Because my soul in grave to dwell
    shall not be left by thee;
Nor wilt thou give thine Holy One
    corruption to see.

11Thou wilt me show the path of life:
    of joys there is full store
Before thy face; at thy right hand
    are pleasures evermore.

Psalm 17

A Prayer of David.

8,6,8,6

1Lord, hear the right, attend my cry,
    unto my pray'r give heed,
That doth not in hypocrisy
    from feigned lips proceed.

2And from before thy presence forth
    my sentence do thou send:
Toward these things that equal are
    do thou thine eyes intend.

3Thou prov'dst mine heart, thou visit'dst me
    by night, thou didst me try,
Yet nothing found'st; for that my mouth
    shall not sin, purposed I.

4As for men's works, I, by the word
    that from thy lips doth flow,
Did me preserve out of the paths
    wherein destroyers go.

5Hold up my goings, Lord, me guide
    in those thy paths divine,

So that my footsteps may not slide
   out of those ways of thine.

[6]I called have on thee, O God,
   because thou wilt me hear:
That thou may'st hearken to my speech,
   to me incline thine ear.

[7]Thy wondrous loving-kindness show,
   thou that, by thy right hand,
Sav'st them that trust in thee from those
   that up against them stand.

[8]As th' apple of the eye me keep;
   in thy wings shade me close
[9]From lewd oppressors, compassing
   me round, as deadly foes.

[10]In their own fat they are inclosed;
   their mouth speaks loftily.
[11]Our steps they compassed; and to ground
   down bowing set their eye.

[12]He like unto a lion is
   that's greedy of his prey,
Or lion young, which lurking doth
   in secret places stay.

[13]Arise, and disappoint my foe,
   and cast him down, O Lord:
My soul save from the wicked man,
   the man which is thy sword.

[14]From men, which are thy hand, O Lord,
   from worldly men me save,
Which only in this present life
   their part and portion have.

Whose belly with thy treasure hid
   thou fill'st: they children have
In plenty; of their goods the rest
   they to their children leave.

¹⁵But as for me, I thine own face
  in righteousness will see;
And with thy likeness, when I wake,
  I satisfied shall be.

Psalm 18

*To the chief Musician, A Psalm of David, the servant of
the Lord, who spake unto the Lord the words of this song
in the day that the Lord delivered him from the hand of all
his enemies, and from the hand of Saul: And he said,*

8,6,8,6

¹Thee will I love, O Lord, my strength.
  ²My fortress is the Lord,
My rock, and he that doth to me
  deliverance afford:

My God, my strength, whom I will trust,
  a buckler unto me,
The horn of my salvation,
  and my high tow'r, is he.

³Upon the Lord, who worthy is
  of praises, will I cry;
And then shall I preserved be
  safe from mine enemy.

⁴Floods of ill men affrighted me,
  death's pangs about me went;
⁵Hell's sorrows me environed;
  death's snares did me prevent.

⁶In my distress I called on God,
  cry to my God did I;
He from his temple heard my voice,
  to his ears came my cry.

⁷Th' earth, as affrighted, then did shake,
  trembling upon it seized:
The hills' foundations moved were,
  because he was displeased.

⁸Up from his nostrils came a smoke,
  and from his mouth there came

Devouring fire, and coals by it
    were turned into flame.

⁹He also bowed down the heav'ns,
    and thence he did descend;
And thickest clouds of darkness did
    under his feet attend.

¹⁰And he upon a cherub rode,
    and thereon he did fly;
Yea, on the swift wings of the wind
    his flight was from on high.

¹¹He darkness made his secret place:
    about him, for his tent,
Dark waters were, and thickest clouds
    of th' airy firmament.

¹²And at the brightness of that light,
    which was before his eye,
His thick clouds passed away, hailstones
    and coals of fire did fly.

¹³The Lord God also in the heav'ns
    did thunder in his ire;
And there the Highest gave his voice,
    hailstones and coals of fire.

¹⁴Yea, he his arrows sent abroad,
    and them he scattered;
His lightnings also he shot out,
    and them discomfited.

¹⁵The waters' channels then were seen,
    the world's foundations vast
At thy rebuke discovered were,
    and at thy nostrils' blast.

¹⁶And from above the Lord sent down,
    and took me from below;
From many waters he me drew,
    which would me overflow.

¹⁷He me relieved from my strong foes,
    and such as did me hate;

Because he saw that they for me
   too strong were, and too great.

18They me prevented in the day
   of my calamity;
But even then the Lord himself
   a stay was unto me.

19He to a place where liberty
   and room was hath me brought;
Because he took delight in me,
   he my deliv'rance wrought.

20According to my righteousness
   he did me recompense,
He me repaid according to
   my hands' pure innocence.

21For I God's ways kept, from my God
   did not turn wickedly.
22His judgments were before me, I
   his laws put not from me.

23Sincere before him was my heart;
   with him upright was I;
And watchfully I kept myself
   from mine iniquity.

24After my righteousness the Lord
   hath recompensed me,
After the cleanness of my hands
   appearing in his eye.

25Thou gracious to the gracious art,
   to upright men upright:
26Pure to the pure, froward thou kyth'st
   unto the froward wight.

27For thou wilt the afflicted save
   in grief that low do lie:
But wilt bring down the countenance
   of them whose looks are high.

28The Lord will light my candle so,
   that it shall shine full bright:

The Lord my God will also make
  my darkness to be light.

29By thee through troops of men I break,
  and them discomfit all;
And, by my God assisting me,
  I overleap a wall.

30As for God, perfect is his way:
  the Lord his word is tried;
He is a buckler to all those
  who do in him confide.

31Who but the Lord is God? but he
  who is a rock and stay?
32'Tis God that girdeth me with strength,
  and perfect makes my way.

33He made my feet swift as the hinds',
  set me on my high places.
34Mine hands to war he taught, mine arms
  brake bows of steel in pieces.

35The shield of thy salvation
  thou didst on me bestow:
Thy right hand held me up, and great
  thy kindness made me grow.

36And in my way my steps thou hast
  enlarged under me,
That I go safely, and my feet
  are kept from sliding free.

37Mine en'mies I pursued have,
  and did them overtake;
Nor did I turn again till I
  an end of them did make.

38I wounded them, they could not rise;
  they at my feet did fall.
39Thou girdedst me with strength for war;
  my foes thou brought'st down all:

40And thou hast giv'n to me the necks
  of all mine enemies;

That I might them destroy and slay,
    who did against me rise.

[41]They cried out, but there was none
    that would or could them save;
Yea, they did cry unto the Lord,
    but he no answer gave.

[42]Then did I beat them small as dust
    before the wind that flies;
And I did cast them out like dirt
    upon the street that lies.

[43]Thou mad'st me free from people's strife,
    and heathen's head to be:
A people whom I have not known
    shall service do to me.

[44]At hearing they shall me obey,
    to me they shall submit.
[45]Strangers for fear shall fade away,
    who in close places sit.

[46]God lives, blessed be my Rock; the God
    of my health praised be.
[47]God doth avenge me, and subdues
    the people under me.

[48]He saves me from mine enemies;
    yea, thou hast lifted me
Above my foes; and from the man
    of vi'lence set me free.

[49]Therefore to thee will I give thanks
    the heathen folk among;
And to thy name, O Lord, I will
    sing praises in a song.

[50]He great deliv'rance gives his king:
    he mercy doth extend
To David, his anointed one,
    and his seed without end.

Psalm 19

To the chief Musician, A Psalm of David.

8,6,8,6

[1]The heav'ns God's glory do declare,
   the skies his hand-works preach:
[2]Day utters speech to day, and night
   to night doth knowledge teach.

[3]There is no speech nor tongue to which
   their voice doth not extend:
[4]Their line is gone through all the earth,
   their words to the world's end.

In them he set the sun a tent;
   [5]Who, bridegroom-like, forth goes
From's chamber, as a strong man doth
   to run his race rejoice.

[6]From heav'n's end is his going forth,
   circling to th' end again;
And there is nothing from his heat
   that hidden doth remain.

[7]God's law is perfect, and converts
   the soul in sin that lies:
God's testimony is most sure,
   and makes the simple wise.

[8]The statutes of the Lord are right,
   and do rejoice the heart:
The Lord's command is pure, and doth
   light to the eyes impart.

[9]Unspotted is the fear of God,
   and doth endure for ever:
The judgments of the Lord are true
   and righteous altogether.

[10]They more than gold, yea, much fine gold,
   to be desired are:
Than honey, honey from the comb
   that droppeth, sweeter far.

[11]Moreover, they thy servant warn
   how he his life should frame:
A great reward provided is
   for them that keep the same.

[12]Who can his errors understand?
   O cleanse thou me within
[13]From secret faults. Thy servant keep
   from all presumptuous sin:

And do not suffer them to have
   dominion over me:
Then, righteous and innocent,
   I from much sin shall be.

[14]The words which from my mouth proceed,
   the thoughts sent from my heart,
Accept, O Lord, for thou my strength
   and my Redeemer art.

Psalm 20

To the chief Musician, A Psalm of David.

8,6,8,6

[1]Jehovah hear thee in the day
   when trouble he doth send:
And let the name of Jacob's God
   thee from all ill defend.

[2]O let him help send from above,
   out of his sanctuary:
From Zion, his own holy hill,
   let him give strength to thee.

[3]Let him remember all thy gifts,
   accept thy sacrifice:
[4]Grant thee thine heart's wish, and fulfill
   thy thoughts and counsel wise.

[5]In thy salvation we will joy;
   in our God's name we will
Display our banners: and the Lord
   thy prayers all fulfill.

⁶Now know I God his king doth save:
 he from his holy heav'n
Will hear him, with the saving strength
 by his own right hand giv'n.

⁷In chariots some put confidence,
 some horses trust upon:
But we remember will the name
 of our Lord God alone.

⁸We rise, and upright stand, when they
 are bowed down, and fall.
⁹Deliver, Lord; and let the King
 us hear, when we do call.

Psalm 21

To the chief Musician, A Psalm of David.

8,6,8,6

¹The king in thy great strength, O Lord,
 shall very joyful be:
In thy salvation rejoice
 how veh'mently shall he!

²Thou hast bestowed upon him
 all that his heart would have;
And thou from him didst not withhold
 whate'er his lips did crave.

³For thou with blessings him prevent'st
 of goodness manifold;
And thou hast set upon his head
 a crown of purest gold.

⁴When he desired life of thee,
 thou life to him didst give;
Ev'n such a length of days, that he
 for evermore should live.

⁵In that salvation wrought by thee
 his glory is made great;
Honour and comely majesty
 thou hast upon him set.

⁶Because that thou for evermore
 most blessed hast him made;
And thou hast with thy countenance
 made him exceeding glad.

⁷Because the king upon the Lord
 his confidence doth lay;
And through the grace of the most High
 shall not be moved away.

⁸Thine hand shall all those men find out
 that en'mies are to thee;
Ev'n thy right hand shall find out those
 of thee that haters be.

⁹Like fiery ov'n thou shalt them make,
 when kindled is thine ire;
God shall them swallow in his wrath,
 devour them shall the fire.

¹⁰Their fruit from earth thou shalt destroy,
 their seed men from among;
¹¹For they beyond their might 'gainst thee
 did plot mischief and wrong.

¹²Thou therefore shalt make them turn back,
 when thou thy shafts shalt place
Upon thy strings, made ready all
 to fly against their face.

¹³In thy great pow'r and strength, O Lord,
 be thou exalted high;
So shall we sing with joyful hearts,
 thy power praise shall we.

Psalm 22

*To the chief Musician upon Aijeleth Shahar, A Psalm of
David.*

8,6,8,6

¹My God, my God, why hast thou me
 forsaken? why so far
Art thou from helping me, and from
 my words that roaring are?

²All day, my God, to thee I cry,
    yet am not heard by thee;
And in the season of the night
    I cannot silent be.

³But thou art holy, thou that dost
    inhabit Isr'el's praise.
⁴Our fathers hoped in thee, they hoped
    and thou didst them release.

⁵When unto thee they sent their cry,
    to them deliv'rance came:
Because they put their trust in thee,
    they were not put to shame.

⁶But as for me, a worm I am,
    and as no man am prized:
Reproach of men I am, and by
    the people am despised.

⁷All that me see laugh me to scorn;
    shoot out the lip do they;
They nod and shake their heads at me,
    and, mocking, thus do say,

⁸This man did trust in God, that he
    would free him by his might:
Let him deliver him, sith he
    had in him such delight.

⁹But thou art he out of the womb
    that didst me safely take;
When I was on my mother's breasts
    thou me to hope didst make.

¹⁰And I was cast upon thy care,
    ev'n from the womb till now;
And from my mother's belly, Lord,
    my God and guide art thou.

¹¹Be not far off, for grief is near,
    and none to help is found.
¹²Bulls many compass me, strong bulls
    of Bashan me surround.

¹³Their mouths they opened wide on me,
    upon me gape did they,
Like to a lion ravening
    and roaring for his prey.

¹⁴Like water I'm poured out, my bones
    all out of joint do part:
Amidst my bowels, as the wax,
    so melted is my heart.

¹⁵My strength is like a potsherd dried;
    my tongue it cleaveth fast
Unto my jaws; and to the dust
    of death thou brought me hast.

¹⁶For dogs have compassed me about:
    the wicked, that did meet
In their assembly, me inclosed;
    they pierced my hands and feet.

¹⁷I all my bones may tell; they do
    upon me look and stare.
¹⁸Upon my vesture lots they cast,
    and clothes among them share.

¹⁹But be not far, O Lord, my strength;
    haste to give help to me.
²⁰From sword my soul, from pow'r of dogs
    my darling set thou free.

²¹Out of the roaring lion's mouth
    do thou me shield and save:
For from the horns of unicorns
    an ear to me thou gave.

²²I will shew forth thy name unto
    those that my brethren are;
Amidst the congregation
    thy praise I will declare.

²³Praise ye the Lord, who do him fear;
    him glorify all ye
The seed of Jacob: fear him all
    that Isr'el's children be.

²⁴For he despised not nor abhorred
    th' afflicted's misery;
Nor from him hid his face, but heard
    when he to him did cry.

²⁵Within the congregation great
    my praise shall be of thee;
My vows before them that him fear
    shall be performed by me.

²⁶The meek shall eat, and shall be filled;
    they also praise shall give
Unto the Lord that do him seek:
    your heart shall ever live.

²⁷All ends of th' earth remember shall,
    and turn the Lord unto;
All kindreds of the nations
    to him shall homage do:

²⁸Because the kingdom to the Lord
    doth appertain as his;
Likewise among the nations
    the Governor he is.

²⁹Earth's fat ones eat, and worship shall:
    all who to dust descend
Shall bow to him; none of them can
    his soul from death defend.

³⁰A seed shall service do to him;
    unto the Lord it shall
Be for a generation
    reckoned in ages all.

³¹They shall come, and they shall declare
    his truth and righteousness
Unto a people yet unborn,
    and that he hath done this.

Psalm 23

A Psalm of David.

8,6,8,6

[1]The Lord's my shepherd, I'll not want.
   [2]He maketh me down to lie
In pastures green: he leadeth me
   the quiet waters by.

[3]My soul he doth restore again;
   and me to walk doth make
Within the paths of righteousness,
   ev'n for his own name's sake.

[4]Yea, though I walk in death's dark vale,
   yet will I fear none ill:
For thou art with me; and thy rod
   and staff me comfort still.

[5]My table thou hast furnished
   in presence of my foes;
My head thou dost with oil anoint,
   and my cup overflows.

[6]Goodness and mercy all my life
   shall surely follow me:
And in God's house for evermore
   my dwelling-place shall be.

Psalm 24

8,6,8,6

[1]The earth belongs unto the Lord,
   and all that it contains;
The world that is inhabited,
   and all that there remains.

[2]For the foundations thereof
   he on the seas did lay,
And he hath it established
   upon the floods to stay.

[3]Who is the man that shall ascend
   into the hill of God?
Or who within his holy place
   shall have a firm abode?

⁴Whose hands are clean, whose heart is pure,
   and unto vanity
Who hath not lifted up his soul,
   nor sworn deceitfully.

⁵He from th' Eternal shall receive
   the blessing him upon,
And righteousness, ev'n from the God
   of his salvation.

⁶This is the generation
   that after him enquire,
O Jacob, who do seek thy face
   with their whole heart's desire.

⁷Ye gates, lift up your heads on high;
   ye doors that last for aye,
Be lifted up, that so the King
   of glory enter may.

⁸But who of glory is the King?
   The mighty Lord is this;
Ev'n that same Lord, that great in might
   and strong in battle is.

⁹Ye gates, lift up your heads; ye doors,
   doors that do last for aye,
Be lifted up, that so the King
   of glory enter may.

¹⁰But who is he that is the King
   of glory? who is this?
The Lord of hosts, and none but he,
   the King of glory is.

Psalm 25

A Psalm of David.

First Version (S.M.)
6,6,8,6

¹To thee I lift my soul:
   ²O Lord, I trust in thee:
My God, let me not be ashamed,
   nor foes triumph o'er me.

³Let none that wait on thee
    be put to shame at all;
But those that without cause transgress,
    let shame upon them fall.

⁴Show me thy ways, O Lord;
    thy paths, O teach thou me:
⁵And do thou lead me in thy truth,
    therein my teacher be:

For thou art God that dost
    to me salvation send,
And I upon thee all the day
    expecting do attend.

⁶Thy tender mercies, Lord,
    I pray thee to remember,
And loving-kindnesses; for they
    have been of old for ever.

⁷My sins and faults of youth
    do thou, O Lord, forget:
After thy mercy think on me,
    and for thy goodness great.

⁸God good and upright is:
    the way he'll sinners show.
⁹The meek in judgment he will guide,
    and make his path to know.

¹⁰The whole paths of the Lord
    are truth and mercy sure,
To those that do his cov'nant keep,
    and testimonies pure.

¹¹Now, for thine own name's sake,
    O Lord, I thee entreat
To pardon mine iniquity;
    for it is very great.

¹²What man is he that fears
    the Lord, and doth him serve?
Him shall he teach the way that he
    shall choose, and still observe.

[13]His soul shall dwell at ease;
   and his posterity
Shall flourish still, and of the earth
   inheritors shall be.

[14]With those that fear him is
   the secret of the Lord;
The knowledge of his covenant
   he will to them afford.

[15]Mine eyes upon the Lord
   continually are set:
For he it is that shall bring forth
   my feet out of the net.

[16]Turn unto me thy face,
   and to me mercy show;
Because that I am desolate,
   and am brought very low.

[17]My heart's griefs are increased:
   me from distress relieve.
[18]See mine affliction and my pain,
   and all my sins forgive.

[19]Consider thou my foes,
   because they many are;
And it a cruel hatred is
   which they against me bear.

[20]O do thou keep my soul,
   do thou deliver me:
And let me never be ashamed,
   because I trust in thee.

[21]Let uprightness and truth
   keep me, who thee attend.
[22]Redemption, Lord, to Israel
   from all his troubles send.

Psalm 25

Second Version (C.M.)
8,6,8,6

[1]To thee I lift my soul, O Lord:
   [2]My God, I trust in thee:
Let me not be ashamed; let not
   my foes triumph o'er me.

[3]Yea, let thou none ashamed be
   that do on thee attend:
Ashamed let them be, O Lord,
   who without cause offend.

[4]Thy ways, Lord, show; teach me thy paths:
   [5]Lead me in truth, teach me:
For of my safety thou art God;
   all day I wait on thee.

[6]Thy mercies, that most tender are,
   do thou, O Lord, remember,
And loving-kindnesses; for they
   have been of old for ever.

[7]Let not the errors of my youth,
   nor sins, remembered be:
In mercy, for thy goodness' sake,
   O Lord, remember me.

[8]The Lord is good and gracious,
   he upright is also:
He therefore sinners will instruct
   in ways that they should go.

[9]The meek and lowly he will guide
   in judgment just alway:
To meek and poor afflicted ones
   he'll clearly teach his way.

[10]The whole paths of the Lord our God
   are truth and mercy sure,
To such as keep his covenant,
   and testimonies pure.

[11]Now, for thine own name's sake, O Lord,
    I humbly thee entreat
To pardon mine iniquity;
    for it is very great.

[12]What man fears God? him shall he teach
    the way that he shall choose.
[13]His soul shall dwell at ease; his seed
    the earth, as heirs, shall use.

[14]The secret of the Lord is with
    such as do fear his name;
And he his holy covenant
    will manifest to them.

[15]Towards the Lord my waiting eyes
    continually are set;
For he it is that shall bring forth
    my feet out of the net.

[16]O turn thee unto me, O God,
    have mercy me upon;
Because I solitary am,
    and in affliction.

[17]Enlarged the griefs are of mine heart;
    me from distress relieve.
[18]See mine affliction and my pain,
    and all my sins forgive.

[19]Consider thou mine enemies,
    because they many are;
And it a cruel hatred is
    which they against me bear.

[20]O do thou keep my soul; O God,
    do thou deliver me:
Let me not be ashamed; for I
    do put my trust in thee.

[21]O let integrity and truth
    keep me, who thee attend.
[22]Redemption, Lord, to Israel
    from all his troubles send.

Psalm 26

A Psalm of David.

8,6,8,6

¹Judge me, O Lord, for I have walked
  in mine integrity:
I trusted also in the Lord;
  slide therefore shall not I.

²Examine me, and do me prove;
  try heart and reins, O God:
³For thy love is before mine eyes,
  thy truth's paths I have trod.

⁴With persons vain I have not sat,
  nor with dissemblers gone:
⁵Th' assembly of ill men I hate;
  to sit with such I shun.

⁶Mine hands in innocence, O Lord,
  I'll wash and purify;
So to thine holy altar go,
  and compass it will I:

⁷That I, with voice of thanksgiving,
  may publish and declare,
And tell of all thy mighty works,
  that great and wondrous are.

⁸The habitation of thy house,
  Lord, I have loved well;
Yea, in that place I do delight
  where doth thine honour dwell.

⁹With sinners gather not my soul,
  and such as blood would spill:
¹⁰Whose hands mischievous plots, right hand
  corrupting bribes do fill.

¹¹But as for me, I will walk on
  in mine integrity:
Do thou redeem me, and, O Lord,
  be merciful to me.

¹²My foot upon an even place
    doth stand with steadfastness:
Within the congregations
    th' Eternal I will bless.

Psalm 27

A Psalm of David.

8,6,8,6

¹The Lord's my light and saving health,
    who shall make me dismayed?
My life's strength is the Lord, of whom
    then shall I be afraid?

²When as mine enemies and foes,
    most wicked persons all,
To eat my flesh against me rose,
    they stumbled and did fall.

³Against me though an host encamp,
    my heart yet fearless is:
Though war against me rise, I will
    be confident in this.

⁴One thing I of the Lord desired,
    and will seek to obtain,
That all days of my life I may
    within God's house remain;

That I the beauty of the Lord
    behold may and admire,
And that I in his holy place
    may rev'rently enquire.

⁵For he in his pavilion shall
    me hide in evil days;
In secret of his tent me hide,
    and on a rock me raise.

⁶And now, ev'n at this present time,
    mine head shall lifted be
Above all those that are my foes,
    and round encompass me:

Therefore unto his tabernacle
    I'll sacrifices bring
Of joyfulness; I'll sing, yea, I
    to God will praises sing.

7O Lord, give ear unto my voice,
    when I do cry to thee;
Upon me also mercy have,
    and do thou answer me.

8When thou didst say, Seek ye my face,
    then unto thee reply
Thus did my heart, Above all things
    thy face, Lord, seek will I.

9Far from me hide not thou thy face;
    put not away from thee
Thy servant in thy wrath: thou hast
    an helper been to me.

O God of my salvation,
    leave me not, nor forsake:
10Though me my parents both should leave,
    the Lord will me up take.

11O Lord, instruct me in thy way,
    to me a leader be
In a plain path, because of those
    that hatred bear to me.

12Give me not to mine en'mies' will;
    for witnesses that lie
Against me risen are, and such
    as breathe out cruelty.

13I fainted had, unless that I
    believed had to see
The Lord's own goodness in the land
    of them that living be.

14Wait on the Lord, and be thou strong,
    and he shall strength afford
Unto thine heart; yea, do thou wait,
    I say, upon the Lord.

Psalm 28

A Psalm of David.

8,6,8,6

¹To thee I'll cry, O Lord, my rock;
    hold not thy peace to me;
Lest like those that to pit descend
    I by thy silence be.

²The voice hear of my humble pray'rs,
    when unto thee I cry;
When to thine holy oracle
    I lift mine hands on high.

³With ill men draw me not away
    that work iniquity;
That speak peace to their friends, while in
    their hearts doth mischief lie.

⁴Give them according to their deeds
    and ills endeavoured:
And as their handy-works deserve,
    to them be rendered.

⁵God shall not build, but them destroy,
    who would not understand
The Lord's own works, nor did regard
    the doing of his hand.

⁶For ever blessed be the Lord,
    for graciously he heard
The voice of my petitions,
    and prayers did regard.

⁷The Lord's my strength and shield; my heart
    upon him did rely;
And I am helped: hence my heart
    doth joy exceedingly,

And with my song I will him praise.
    ⁸Their strength is God alone:
He also is the saving strength
    of his anointed one.

⁹O thine own people do thou save,
   bless thine inheritance;
Them also do thou feed, and them
   for evermore advance.

Psalm 29

A Psalm of David.

8,6,8,6

¹Give ye unto the Lord, ye sons
   that of the mighty be,
All strength and glory to the Lord
   with cheerfulness give ye.

²Unto the Lord the glory give
   that to his name is due;
And in the beauty of holiness
   unto Jehovah bow.

³The Lord's voice on the waters is;
   the God of majesty
Doth thunder, and on multitudes
   of waters sitteth he.

⁴A pow'rful voice it is that comes
   out from the Lord most high;
The voice of that great Lord is full
   of glorious majesty.

⁵The voice of the Eternal doth
   asunder cedars tear;
Yea, God the Lord doth cedars break
   that Lebanon doth bear.

⁶He makes them like a calf to skip,
   ev'n that great Lebanon,
And, like to a young unicorn,
   the mountain Sirion.

⁷God's voice divides the flames of fire;
   ⁸The desert it doth shake:
The Lord doth make the wilderness
   of Kadesh all to quake.

⁹God's voice doth make the hinds to calve,
　　it makes the forest bare:
And in his temple ev'ry one
　　his glory doth declare.

¹⁰The Lord sits on the floods; the Lord
　　sits King, and ever shall.
¹¹The Lord will give his people strength,
　　and with peace bless them all.

Psalm 30

A Psalm and Song at the dedication of the house of David.

8,6,8,6

¹Lord, I will thee extol, for thou
　　hast lifted me on high,
And over me thou to rejoice
　　mad'st not mine enemy.

²O thou who art the Lord my God,
　　I in distress to thee,
With loud cries lifted up my voice,
　　and thou hast healed me.

³O Lord, my soul thou hast brought up,
　　and rescued from the grave;
That I to pit should not go down,
　　alive thou didst me save.

⁴O ye that are his holy ones,
　　sing praise unto the Lord;
And give unto him thanks, when ye
　　his holiness record.

⁵For but a moment lasts his wrath;
　　life in his favour lies:
Weeping may for a night endure,
　　at morn doth joy arise.

⁶In my prosperity I said,
　　that nothing shall me move.
⁷O Lord, thou hast my mountain made
　　to stand strong by thy love:

But when that thou, O gracious God,
   didst hide thy face from me,
Then quickly was my prosp'rous state
   turned into misery.

[8]Wherefore unto the Lord my cry
   I caused to ascend:
My humble supplication
   I to the Lord did send.

[9]What profit is there in my blood,
   when I go down to pit?
Shall unto thee the dust give praise?
   thy truth declare shall it?

[10]Hear, Lord, have mercy; help me, Lord:
   [11]Thou turned hast my sadness
To dancing; yea, my sackcloth loosed,
   and girded me with gladness;

[12]That sing thy praise my glory may,
   and never silent be.
O Lord my God, for evermore
   I will give thanks to thee.

Psalm 31

To the chief Musician, A Psalm of David.

8,6,8,6

[1]In thee, O Lord, I put my trust,
   shamed let me never be;
According to thy righteousness
   do thou deliver me.

[2]Bow down thine ear to me, with speed
   send me deliverance:
To save me, my strong rock be thou,
   and my house of defence.

[3]Because thou art my rock, and thee
   I for my fortress take;
Therefore do thou me lead and guide,
   ev'n for thine own name's sake.

⁴And sith thou art my strength, therefore
   pull me out of the net,
Which they in subtlety for me
   so privily have set.

⁵Into thine hands I do commit
   my sp'rit: for thou art he,
O thou, Jehovah, God of truth,
   that hast redeemed me.

⁶Those that do lying vanities
   regard, I have abhorred:
But as for me, my confidence
   is fixed on the Lord.

⁷I'll in thy mercy gladly joy:
   for thou my miseries
Considered hast; thou hast my soul
   known in adversities:

⁸And thou hast not inclosed me
   within the en'my's hand;
And by thee have my feet been made
   in a large room to stand.

⁹O Lord, upon me mercy have,
   for trouble is on me:
Mine eye, my belly, and my soul,
   with grief consumed be.

¹⁰Because my life with grief is spent,
   my years with sighs and groans:
My strength doth fail; and for my sin
   consumed are my bones.

¹¹I was a scorn to all my foes,
   and to my friends a fear;
And specially reproached of those
   that were my neighbours near:

When they me saw they from me fled.
   ¹²Ev'n so I am forgot,
As men are out of mind when dead:
   I'm like a broken pot.

¹³For slanders I of many heard;
   fear compassed me, while they
Against me did consult, and plot
   to take my life away.

¹⁴But as for me, O Lord, my trust
   upon thee I did lay;
And I to thee, Thou art my God,
   did confidently say.

¹⁵My times are wholly in thine hand:
   do thou deliver me
From their hands that mine enemies
   and persecutors be.

¹⁶Thy countenance to shine do thou
   upon thy servant make:
Unto me give salvation,
   for thy great mercies' sake.

¹⁷Let me not be ashamed, O Lord,
   for on thee called I have:
Let wicked men be shamed, let them
   be silent in the grave.

¹⁸To silence put the lying lips,
   that grievous things do say,
And hard reports, in pride and scorn,
   on righteous men do lay.

¹⁹How great's the goodness thou for them
   that fear thee keep'st in store,
And wrought'st for them that trust in thee
   the sons of men before!

²⁰In secret of thy presence thou
   shalt hide them from man's pride:
From strife of tongues thou closely shalt,
   as in a tent, them hide.

²¹All praise and thanks be to the Lord;
   for he hath magnified
His wondrous love to me within
   a city fortified.

[22]For from thine eyes cut off I am,
    I in my haste had said;
My voice yet heard'st thou, when to thee
    with cries my moan I made.

[23]O love the Lord, all ye his saints;
    because the Lord doth guard
The faithful, and he plenteously
    proud doers doth reward.

[24]Be of good courage, and he strength
    unto your heart shall send,
All ye whose hope and confidence
    doth on the Lord depend.

Psalm 32

A Psalm of David, Maschil.

8,6,8,6

[1]O blessed is the man to whom
    is freely pardoned
All the transgression he hath done,
    whose sin is covered.

[2]Blessed is the man to whom the Lord
    imputeth not his sin,
And in whose sp'rit there is no guile,
    nor fraud is found therein.

[3]When as I did refrain my speech,
    and silent was my tongue,
My bones then waxed old, because
    I roared all day long.

[4]For upon me both day and night
    thine hand did heavy lie,
So that my moisture turned is
    in summer's drought thereby.

[5]I thereupon have unto thee
    my sin acknowledged,
And likewise mine iniquity
    I have not covered:

I will confess unto the Lord
    my trespasses, said I;
And of my sin thou freely didst
    forgive th' iniquity.

6For this shall ev'ry godly one
    his prayer make to thee;
In such a time he shall thee seek,
    as found thou mayest be.

Surely, when floods of waters great
    do swell up to the brim,
They shall not overwhelm his soul,
    nor once come near to him.

7Thou art my hiding-place, thou shalt
    from trouble keep me free:
Thou with songs of deliverance
    about shalt compass me.

8I will instruct thee, and thee teach
    the way that thou shalt go;
And, with mine eye upon thee set,
    I will direction show.

9Then be not like the horse or mule,
    which do not understand;
Whose mouth, lest they come near to thee,
    a bridle must command.

10Unto the man that wicked is
    his sorrows shall abound;
But him that trusteth in the Lord
    mercy shall compass round.

11Ye righteous, in the Lord be glad,
    in him do ye rejoice:
All ye that upright are in heart,
    for joy lift up your voice.

Psalm 33

8,6,8,6

¹Ye righteous, in the Lord rejoice;
    it comely is and right,
That upright men, with thankful voice,
    should praise the Lord of might.

²Praise God with harp, and unto him
    sing with the psaltery;
Upon a ten-stringed instrument
    make ye sweet melody.

³A new song to him sing, and play
    with loud noise skilfully;
⁴For right is God's word, all his works
    are done in verity.

⁵To judgment and to righteousness
    a love he beareth still;
The loving-kindness of the Lord
    the earth throughout doth fill.

⁶The heavens by the word of God
    did their beginning take;
And by the breathing of his mouth
    he all their hosts did make.

⁷The waters of the seas he brings
    together as an heap;
And in storehouses, as it were,
    he layeth up the deep.

⁸Let earth, and all that live therein,
    with rev'rence fear the Lord;
Let all the world's inhabitants
    dread him with one accord.

⁹For he did speak the word, and done
    it was without delay;
Established it firmly stood,
    whatever he did say.

¹⁰God doth the counsel bring to nought
    which heathen folk do take;

And what the people do devise
   of none effect doth make.

11O but the counsel of the Lord
   doth stand for ever sure;
And of his heart the purposes
   from age to age endure.

12That nation blessed is, whose God
   Jehovah is, and those
A blessed people are, whom for
   his heritage he chose.

13The Lord from heav'n sees and beholds
   all sons of men full well:
14He views all from his dwelling-place
   that in the earth do dwell.

15He forms their hearts alike, and all
   their doings he observes.
16Great hosts save not a king, much strength
   no mighty man preserves.

17An horse for preservation
   is a deceitful thing;
And by the greatness of his strength
   can no deliv'rance bring.

18Behold on those that do him fear
   the Lord doth set his eye;
Ev'n those who on his mercy do
   with confidence rely.

19From death to free their soul, in dearth
   life unto them to yield.
20Our soul doth wait upon the Lord;
   he is our help and shield.

21Sith in his holy name we trust,
   our heart shall joyful be.
22Lord, let thy mercy be on us,
   as we do hope in thee.

Psalm 34

A Psalm of David, when he changed his behaviour before
Abimelech; who drove him away, and he departed.

8,6,8,6

¹God will I bless all times; his praise
 my mouth shall still express.
²My soul shall boast in God: the meek
 shall hear with joyfulness.

³Extol the Lord with me, let us
 exalt his name together.
⁴I sought the Lord, he heard, and did
 me from all fears deliver.

⁵They looked to him, and lightened were:
 not shamed were their faces.
⁶This poor man cried, God heard, and saved
 him from all his distresses.

⁷The angel of the Lord encamps,
 and round encompasseth
All those about that do him fear,
 and them delivereth.

⁸O taste and see that God is good:
 who trusts in him is blessed.
⁹Fear God his saints: none that him fear
 shall be with want oppressed.

¹⁰The lions young may hungry be,
 and they may lack their food:
But they that truly seek the Lord
 shall not lack any good.

¹¹O children, hither do ye come,
 and unto me give ear;
I shall you teach to understand
 how ye the Lord should fear.

¹²What man is he that life desires,
 to see good would live long?
¹³Thy lips refrain from speaking guile,
 and from ill words thy tongue.

¹⁴Depart from ill, do good, seek peace,
    pursue it earnestly.
¹⁵God's eyes are on the just; his ears
    are open to their cry.

¹⁶The face of God is set against
    those that do wickedly,
That he may quite out from the earth
    cut off their memory.

¹⁷The righteous cry unto the Lord,
    he unto them gives ear;
And they out of their troubles all
    by him delivered are.

¹⁸The Lord is ever nigh to them
    that be of broken sp'rit;
To them he safety doth afford
    that are in heart contrite.

¹⁹The troubles that afflict the just
    in number many be;
But yet at length out of them all
    the Lord doth set him free.

²⁰He carefully his bones doth keep,
    whatever can befall;
That not so much as one of them
    can broken be at all.

²¹Ill shall the wicked slay; laid waste
    shall be who hate the just.
²²The Lord redeems his servants' souls;
    none perish that him trust.

Psalm 35

A Psalm of David.

8,6,8,6

¹Plead, Lord, with those that plead; and fight
    with those that fight with me.
²Of shield and buckler take thou hold,
    stand up mine help to be.

³Draw also out the spear, and do
   against them stop the way
That me pursue: unto my soul,
   I'm thy salvation, say.

⁴Let them confounded be and shamed
   that for my soul have sought:
Who plot my hurt turned back be they,
   and to confusion brought.

⁵Let them be like unto the chaff
   that flies before the wind;
And let the angel of the Lord
   pursue them hard behind.

⁶With darkness cover thou their way,
   and let it slipp'ry prove;
And let the angel of the Lord
   pursue them from above.

⁷For without cause have they for me
   their net hid in a pit,
They also have without a cause
   for my soul digged it.

⁸Let ruin seize him unawares;
   his net he hid withal
Himself let catch; and in the same
   destruction let him fall.

⁹My soul in God shall joy; and glad
   in his salvation be:
¹⁰And all my bones shall say, O Lord,
   who is like unto thee,

Which dost the poor set free from him
   that is for him too strong;
The poor and needy from the man
   that spoils and does him wrong?

¹¹False witnesses rose; to my charge
   things I not knew they laid.
¹²They, to the spoiling of my soul,
   me ill for good repaid.

[13]But as for me, when they were sick,
   in sackcloth sad I mourned:
My humbled soul did fast, my pray'r
   into my bosom turned.

[14]Myself I did behave as he
   had been my friend or brother;
I heavily bowed down, as one
   that mourneth for his mother.

[15]But in my trouble they rejoiced,
   gath'ring themselves together;
Yea, abjects vile together did
   themselves against me gather:

I knew it not; they did me tear,
   and quiet would not be.
[16]With mocking hypocrites, at feasts
   they gnash'd their teeth at me.

[17]How long, Lord, look'st thou on? from those
   destructions they intend
Rescue my soul, from lions young
   my darling do defend.

[18]I will give thanks to thee, O Lord,
   within th' assembly great;
And where much people gathered are
   thy praises forth will set.

[19]Let not my wrongful enemies
   proudly rejoice o'er me;
Nor who me hate without a cause,
   let them wink with the eye.

[20]For peace they do not speak at all;
   but crafty plots prepare
Against all those within the land
   that meek and quiet are.

[21]With mouths set wide, they 'gainst me said,
   Ha, ha! our eye doth see.
[22]Lord, thou hast seen, hold not thy peace;
   Lord, be not far from me.

23Stir up thyself; wake, that thou may'st
   judgment to me afford,
Ev'n to my cause, O thou that art
   my only God and Lord.

24O Lord my God, do thou me judge
   after thy righteousness;
And let them not their joy 'gainst me
   triumphantly express:

25Nor let them say within their hearts,
   Ah, we would have it thus;
Nor suffer them to say, that he
   is swallowed up by us.

26Shamed and confounded be they all
   that at my hurt are glad;
Let those against me that do boast
   with shame and scorn be clad.

27Let them that love my righteous cause
   be glad, shout, and not cease
To say, The Lord be magnified,
   who loves his servant's peace.

28Thy righteousness shall also be
   declared by my tongue;
The praises that belong to thee
   speak shall it all day long.

Psalm 36

To the chief Musician, A Psalm of David, the servant of
the Lord.

8,6,8,6

1The wicked man's transgression
   within my heart thus says,
Undoubtedly the fear of God
   is not before his eyes.

2Because himself he flattereth
   in his own blinded eye,
Until the hatefulness be found
   of his iniquity.

³Words from his mouth proceeding are,
    fraud and iniquity:
He to be wise, and to do good,
    hath left off utterly.

⁴He mischief, lying on his bed,
    most cunningly doth plot:
He sets himself in ways not good,
    ill he abhorreth not.

⁵Thy mercy, Lord, is in the heav'ns;
    thy truth doth reach the clouds:
⁶Thy justice is like mountains great;
    thy judgments deep as floods:

Lord, thou preservest man and beast.
    ⁷How precious is thy grace!
Therefore in shadow of thy wings
    men's sons their trust shall place.

⁸They with the fatness of thy house
    shall be well satisfied;
From rivers of thy pleasures thou
    wilt drink to them provide.

⁹Because of life the fountain pure
    remains alone with thee;
And in that purest light of thine
    we clearly light shall see.

¹⁰Thy loving-kindness unto them
    continue that thee know;
And still on men upright in heart
    thy righteousness bestow.

¹¹Let not the foot of cruel pride
    come, and against me stand;
And let me not removed be,
    Lord, by the wicked's hand.

¹²There fallen are they, and ruined,
    that work iniquities:
Cast down they are, and never shall
    be able to arise.

Psalm 37

8,6,8,6

A Psalm of David.

[1]For evil-doers fret thou not
  thyself unquietly;
Nor do thou envy bear to those
  that work iniquity.

[2]For, even like unto the grass,
  soon be cut down shall they;
And, like the green and tender herb,
  they wither shall away.

[3]Set thou thy trust upon the Lord,
  and be thou doing good;
And so thou in the land shalt dwell,
  and verily have food.

[4]Delight thyself in God; he'll give
  thine heart's desire to thee.
[5]Thy way to God commit, him trust,
  it bring to pass shall he.

[6]And, like unto the light, he shall
  thy righteousness display;
And he thy judgment shall bring forth
  like noon-tide of the day.

[7]Rest in the Lord, and patiently
  wait for him: do not fret
For him who, prosp'ring in his way,
  success in sin doth get.

[8]Do thou from anger cease, and wrath
  see thou forsake also:
Fret not thyself in any wise,
  that evil thou should'st do.

[9]For those that evil doers are
  shall be cut off and fall:
But those that wait upon the Lord
  the earth inherit shall.

¹⁰For yet a little while, and then
   the wicked shall not be;
His place thou shalt consider well,
   but it thou shalt not see.

¹¹But by inheritance the earth
   the meek ones shall possess:
They also shall delight themselves
   in an abundant peace.

¹²The wicked plots against the just,
   and at him whets his teeth:
¹³The Lord shall laugh at him, because
   his day he coming seeth.

¹⁴The wicked have drawn out the sword,
   and bent their bow, to slay
The poor and needy, and to kill
   men of an upright way.

¹⁵But their own sword, which they have drawn,
   shall enter their own heart:
Their bows which they have bent shall break,
   and into pieces part.

¹⁶A little that a just man hath
   is more and better far
Than is the wealth of many such
   as lewd and wicked are.

¹⁷For sinners' arms shall broken be;
   but God the just sustains.
¹⁸God knows the just man's days, and still
   their heritage remains.

¹⁹They shall not be ashamed when they
   the evil time do see;
And when the days of famine are,
   they satisfied shall be.

²⁰But wicked men, and foes of God,
   as fat of lambs, decay;
They shall consume, yea, into smoke
   they shall consume away.

²¹The wicked borrows, but the same
 again he doth not pay;
Whereas the righteous mercy shows,
 and gives his own away.

²²For such as blessed be of him
 the earth inherit shall;
And they that cursed are of him
 shall be destroyed all.

²³A good man's footsteps by the Lord
 are ordered aright;
And in the way wherein he walks
 he greatly doth delight.

²⁴Although he fall, yet shall he not
 be cast down utterly;
Because the Lord with his own hand
 upholds him mightily.

²⁵I have been young, and now am old,
 yet have I never seen
The just man left, nor that his seed
 for bread have beggars been.

²⁶He's ever merciful, and lends:
 his seed is blessed therefore.
²⁷Depart from evil, and do good,
 and dwell for evermore.

²⁸For God loves judgment, and his saints
 leaves not in any case;
They are kept ever: but cut off
 shall be the sinner's race.

²⁹The just inherit shall the land,
 and ever in it dwell:
³⁰The just man's mouth doth wisdom speak;
 his tongue doth judgment tell.

³¹In's heart the law is of his God,
 his steps slide not away.
³²The wicked man doth watch the just,
 and seeketh him to slay.

³³Yet him the Lord will not forsake,
   nor leave him in his hands:
The righteous will he not condemn,
   when he in judgment stands.

³⁴Wait on the Lord, and keep his way,
   and thee exalt shall he
Th' earth to inherit; when cut off
   the wicked thou shalt see.

³⁵I saw the wicked great in pow'r,
   spread like a green bay-tree:
³⁶He passed, yea, was not; him I sought,
   but found he could not be.

³⁷Mark thou the perfect, and behold
   the man of uprightness;
Because that surely of this man
   the latter end is peace.

³⁸But those men that transgressors are
   shall be destroyed together;
The latter end of wicked men
   shall be cut off for ever.

³⁹But the salvation of the just
   is from the Lord above;
He in the time of their distress
   their stay and strength doth prove.

⁴⁰The Lord shall help, and them deliver:
   he shall them free and save
From wicked men; because in him
   their confidence they have.

Psalm 38

A Psalm of David, to bring to remembrance.

8,6,8,6

¹In thy great indignation,
   O Lord, rebuke me not;
Nor on me lay thy chast'ning hand,
   in thy displeasure hot.

[2]For in me fast thine arrows stick,
    thine hand doth press me sore:
[3]And in my flesh there is no health,
    nor soundness any more.

This grief I have, because thy wrath
    is forth against me gone;
And in my bones there is no rest,
    for sin that I have done.

[4]Because gone up above mine head
    my great transgressions be;
And, as a weighty burden, they
    too heavy are for me.

[5]My wounds do stink, and are corrupt;
    my folly makes it so.
[6]I troubled am, and much bowed down;
    all day I mourning go.

[7]For a disease that loathsome is
    so fills my loins with pain,
That in my weak and weary flesh
    no soundness doth remain.

[8]So feeble and infirm am I,
    and broken am so sore,
That, through disquiet of my heart,
    I have been made to roar.

[9]O Lord, all that I do desire
    is still before thine eye;
And of my heart the secret groans
    not hidden are from thee.

[10]My heart doth pant incessantly,
    my strength doth quite decay;
As for mine eyes, their wonted light
    is from me gone away.

[11]My lovers and my friends do stand
    at distance from my sore;
And those do stand aloof that were
    kinsmen and kind before.

¹²Yea, they that seek my life lay snares:
     who seek to do me wrong
Speak things mischievous, and deceits
     imagine all day long.

¹³But, as one deaf, that heareth not,
     I suffered all to pass;
I as a dumb man did become,
     whose mouth not opened was:

¹⁴As one that hears not, in whose mouth
     are no reproofs at all.
¹⁵For, Lord, I hope in thee; my God,
     thou'lt hear me when I call.

¹⁶For I said, Hear me, lest they should
     rejoice o'er me with pride;
And o'er me magnify themselves,
     when as my foot doth slide.

¹⁷For I am near to halt, my grief
     is still before mine eye:
¹⁸For I'll declare my sin, and grieve
     for mine iniquity.

¹⁹But yet mine en'mies lively are,
     and strong are they beside;
And they that hate me wrongfully
     are greatly multiplied.

²⁰And they for good that render ill,
     as en'mies me withstood;
Yea, ev'n for this, because that I
     do follow what is good.

²¹Forsake me not, O Lord; my God,
     far from me never be.
²²O Lord, thou my salvation art,
     haste to give help to me.

Psalm 39

To the chief Musician, even to Jeduthan, A Psalm of David.

8,6,8,6

1 I said, I will look to my ways,
    lest with my tongue I sin:
In sight of wicked men my mouth
    with bridle I'll keep in.

2 With silence I as dumb became,
    I did myself restrain
From speaking good; but then the more
    increased was my pain.

3 My heart within me waxed hot;
    and, while I musing was,
The fire did burn; and from my tongue
    these words I did let pass:

4 Mine end, and measure of my days,
    O Lord, unto me show
What is the same; that I thereby
    my frailty well may know.

5 Lo, thou my days an handbreadth mad'st;
    mine age is in thine eye
As nothing: sure each man at best
    is wholly vanity.

6 Sure each man walks in a vain show;
    they vex themselves in vain:
He heaps up wealth, and doth not know
    to whom it shall pertain.

7 And now, O Lord, what wait I for?
    my hope is fixed on thee.
8 Free me from all my trespasses,
    the fool's scorn make not me.

9 Dumb was I, op'ning not my mouth,
    because this work was thine.
10 Thy stroke take from me; by the blow
    of thine hand I do pine.

¹¹When with rebukes thou dost correct
   man for iniquity,
Thou wastes his beauty like a moth:
   sure each man's vanity.

¹²Attend my cry, Lord, at my tears
   and pray'rs not silent be:
I sojourn as my fathers all,
   and stranger am with thee.

¹³O spare thou me, that I my strength
   recover may again,
Before from hence I do depart,
   and here no more remain.

Psalm 40

To the chief Musician, A Psalm of David.

8,6,8,6

¹I waited for the Lord my God,
   and patiently did bear;
At length to me he did incline
   my voice and cry to hear.

²He took me from a fearful pit,
   and from the miry clay,
And on a rock he set my feet,
   establishing my way.

³He put a new song in my mouth,
   our God to magnify:
Many shall see it, and shall fear,
   and on the Lord rely.

⁴O blessed is the man whose trust
   upon the Lord relies;
Respecting not the proud, nor such
   as turn aside to lies.

⁵O Lord my God, full many are
   the wonders thou hast done;
Thy gracious thoughts to us-ward far
   above all thoughts are gone:

In order none can reckon them
    to thee: if them declare,
And speak of them I would, they more
    than can be number'd are.

6No sacrifice nor offering
    didst thou at all desire;
Mine ears thou bored: sin-off'ring thou
    and burnt didst not require:

7Then to the Lord these were my words,
    I come, behold and see;
Within the volume of the book
    it written is of me:

8To do thy will I take delight,
    O thou my God that art;
Yea, that most holy law of thine
    I have within my heart.

9Within the congregation great
    I righteousness did preach:
Lo, thou dost know, O Lord, that I
    refrained not my speech.

10I never did within my heart
    conceal thy righteousness;
I thy salvation have declared,
    and shown thy faithfulness:

Thy kindness, which most loving is,
    concealed have not I,
Nor from the congregation great
    have hid thy verity.

11Thy tender mercies, Lord, from me
    O do thou not restrain;
Thy loving-kindness, and thy truth,
    let them me still maintain.

12For ills past reck'ning compass me,
    and mine iniquities
Such hold upon me taken have,
    I cannot lift mine eyes:

They more than hairs are on mine head,
    thence is my heart dismayed.
[13]Be pleased, Lord, to rescue me;
    Lord, hasten to mine aid.

[14]Shamed and confounded be they all
    that seek my soul to kill;
Yea, let them backward driven be,
    and shamed, that wish me ill.

[15]For a reward of this their shame
    confounded let them be.
That in this manner scoffing say,
    Aha, aha! to me.

[16]In thee let all be glad, and joy,
    who seeking thee abide;
Who thy salvation love, say still,
    The Lord be magnified.

[17]I'm poor and needy, yet the Lord
    of me a care doth take:
Thou art my help and saviour,
    my God, no tarrying make.

Psalm 41

To the chief Musician, A Psalm of David.

                                          8,6,8,6

[1]Blessed is he that wisely doth
    the poor man's case consider;
For when the time of trouble is,
    the Lord will him deliver.

[2]God will him keep, yea, save alive;
    on earth he blessed shall live;
And to his enemies' desire
    thou wilt him not up give.

[3]God will give strength when he on bed
    of languishing doth mourn;
And in his sickness sore, O Lord,
    thou all his bed wilt turn.

[4]I said, O Lord, do thou extend
    thy mercy unto me;
O do thou heal my soul; for why?
    I have offended thee.

[5]Those that to me are enemies,
    of me do evil say,
When shall he die, that so his name
    may perish quite away?

[6]To see me if he comes, he speaks
    vain words: but then his heart
Heaps mischief to it, which he tells,
    when forth he doth depart.

[7]My haters jointly whispering,
    'gainst me my hurt devise.
[8]Mischief, say they, cleaves fast to him;
    he li'th, and shall not rise.

[9]Yea, ev'n mine own familiar friend,
    on whom I did rely,
Who ate my bread, ev'n he his heel
    against me lifted high.

[10]But, Lord, be merciful to me,
    and up again me raise,
That I may justly them requite
    according to their ways.

[11]By this I know that certainly
    I favoured am by thee;
Because my hateful enemy
    triumphs not over me.

[12]But as for me, thou me uphold'st
    in mine integrity;
And me before thy countenance
    thou sett'st continually.

[13]The Lord, the God of Israel,
    be blessed for ever then,
From age to age eternally.
    Amen, yea, and amen.

Psalm 42

To the chief Musician, Maschil, for the sons of Korah.

8,6,8,6

¹Like as the hart for water-brooks
    in thirst doth pant and bray;
So pants my longing soul, O God,
    that come to thee I may.

²My soul for God, the living God,
    doth thirst: when shall I near
Unto thy countenance approach,
    and in God's sight appear?

³My tears have unto me been meat,
    both in the night and day,
While unto me continually,
    Where is thy God? they say.

⁴My soul is poured out in me,
    when this I think upon;
Because that with the multitude
    I heretofore had gone:

With them into God's house I went,
    with voice of joy and praise;
Yea, with the multitude that kept
    the solemn holy days.

⁵O why art thou cast down, my soul?
    why in me so dismayed?
Trust God, for I shall praise him yet,
    his count'nance is mine aid.

⁶My God, my soul's cast down in me;
    thee therefore mind I will
From Jordan's land, the Hermonites,
    and ev'n from Mizar hill.

⁷At the noise of thy water-spouts
    deep unto deep doth call;
Thy breaking waves pass over me,
    yea, and thy billows all.

[8]His loving-kindness yet the Lord
   command will in the day,
His song's with me by night; to God,
   by whom I live, I'll pray:

[9]And I will say to God my rock,
   Why me forgett'st thou so?
Why, for my foes' oppression,
   thus mourning do I go?

[10]'Tis as a sword within my bones,
   when my foes me upbraid;
Ev'n when by them, Where is thy God?
   'tis daily to me said.

[11]O why art thou cast down, my soul?
   why, thus with grief oppressed,
Art thou disquieted in me?
   in God still hope and rest:

For yet I know I shall him praise,
   who graciously to me
The health is of my countenance,
   yea, mine own God is he.

Psalm 43

8,6,8,6

[1]Judge me, O God, and plead my cause
   against th' ungodly nation;
From the unjust and crafty man,
   O be thou my salvation.

[2]For thou the God art of my strength;
   why thrusts thou me thee fro'?
For th' enemy's oppression
   why do I mourning go?

[3]O send thy light forth and thy truth;
   let them be guides to me,
And bring me to thine holy hill,
   ev'n where thy dwellings be.

[4]Then will I to God's altar go,
   to God my chiefest joy:

Yea, God, my God, thy name to praise
    my harp I will employ.

5Why art thou then cast down, my soul?
    what should discourage thee?
And why with vexing thoughts art thou
    disquieted in me?

Still trust in God; for him to praise
    good cause I yet shall have:
He of my count'nance is the health,
    my God that doth me save.

Psalm 44

To the chief Musician for the sons of Korah, Maschil.

8,6,8,6

1O God, we with our ears have heard,
    our fathers have us told,
What works thou in their days hadst done,
    ev'n in the days of old.

2Thy hand did drive the heathen out,
    and plant them in their place;
Thou didst afflict the nations,
    but them thou didst increase.

3For neither got their sword the land,
    nor did their arm them save;
But thy right hand, arm, countenance;
    for thou them favour gave.

4Thou art my King: for Jacob, Lord,
    deliv'rances command.
5Through thee we shall push down our foes,
    that do against us stand:

We, through thy name, shall tread down those
    that ris'n against us have.
6For in my bow I shall not trust,
    nor shall my sword me save.

7But from our foes thou hast us saved,
    our haters put to shame.

[8]In God we all the day do boast,
    and ever praise thy name.

[9]But now we are cast off by thee,
    and us thou putt'st to shame;
And when our armies do go forth,
    thou go'st not with the same.

[10]Thou mak'st us from the enemy,
    faint-hearted, to turn back;
And they who hate us for themselves
    our spoils away do take.

[11]Like sheep for meat thou gavest us;
    'mong heathen cast we be.
[12]Thou didst for nought thy people sell;
    their price enriched not thee.

[13]Thou mak'st us a reproach to be
    unto our neighbours near;
Derision and a scorn to them
    that round about us are.

[14]A by-word also thou dost us
    among the heathen make;
The people, in contempt and spite,
    at us their heads do shake.

[15]Before me my confusion
    continually abides;
And of my bashful countenance
    the shame me ever hides:

[16]For voice of him that doth reproach,
    and speaketh blasphemy;
By reason of th' avenging foe,
    and cruel enemy.

[17]All this is come on us, yet we
    have not forgotten thee;
Nor falsely in thy covenant
    behaved ourselves have we.

[18]Back from thy way our heart not turned;
    our steps no straying made;

[19]Though us thou brak'st in dragons' place,
    and cover'dst with death's shade.

[20]If we God's name forgot, or stretched
    to a strange god our hands,
[21]Shall not God search this out? for he
    heart's secrets understands.

[22]Yea, for thy sake we're killed all day,
    counted as slaughter-sheep.
[23]Rise, Lord, cast us not ever off;
    awake, why dost thou sleep?

[24]O wherefore hidest thou thy face?
    forgett'st our cause distressed,
[25]And our oppression? For our soul
    is to the dust down pressed:

Our belly also on the earth
    fast cleaving, hold doth take.
[26]Rise for our help, and us redeem,
    ev'n for thy mercies' sake.

Psalm 45

To the chief Musician upon Shoshannim, for the sons of
Korah, Maschil, A Song of loves.

First Version (C.M.)
8,6,8,6

[1]My heart brings forth a goodly thing;
    my words that I indite
Concern the King: my tongue's a pen
    of one that swift doth write.

[2]Thou fairer art than sons of men:
    into thy lips is store
Of grace infused; God therefore thee
    hath blessed for evermore.

[3]O thou that art the mighty One,
    thy sword gird on thy thigh;
Ev'n with thy glory excellent,
    and with thy majesty.

⁴For meekness, truth, and righteousness,
    in state ride prosp'rously;
And thy right hand shall thee instruct
    in things that fearful be.

⁵Thine arrows sharply pierce the heart
    of th' en'mies of the King;
And under thy subjection
    the people down do bring.

⁶For ever and for ever is,
    O God, thy throne of might;
The sceptre of thy kingdom is
    a sceptre that is right.

⁷Thou lovest right, and hatest ill;
    for God, thy God, most high,
Above thy fellows hath with th' oil
    of joy anointed thee.

⁸Of aloes, myrrh, and cassia,
    a smell thy garments had,
Out of the iv'ry palaces,
    whereby they made thee glad.

⁹Among thy women honourable
    kings' daughters were at hand:
Upon thy right hand did the queen
    in gold of Ophir stand.

¹⁰O daughter, hearken and regard,
    and do thine ear incline;
Likewise forget thy father's house,
    and people that are thine.

¹¹Then of the King desired shall be
    thy beauty veh'mently:
Because he is thy Lord, do thou
    him worship rev'rently.

¹²The daughter there of Tyre shall be
    with gifts and off'rings great:
Those of the people that are rich
    thy favour shall entreat.

[13]Behold, the daughter of the King
    all glorious is within;
And with embroideries of gold
    her garments wrought have been.

[14]She shall be brought unto the King
    in robes with needle wrought;
Her fellow-virgins following
    shall unto thee be brought.

[15]They shall be brought with gladness great,
    and mirth on ev'ry side,
Into the palace of the King,
    and there they shall abide.

[16]Instead of those thy fathers dear,
    thy children thou may'st take,
And in all places of the earth
    them noble princes make.

[17]Thy name remember'd I will make
    through ages all to be:
The people therefore evermore
    shall praises give to thee.

Psalm 45

Second Version (S.M.)
6,6,8,6

[1]My heart inditing is
    good matter in a song:
I speak the things that I have made,
    which to the King belong:

My tongue shall be as quick,
    his honour to indite,
As is the pen of any scribe
    that useth fast to write.

[2]Thou'rt fairest of all men;
    grace in thy lips doth flow:
And therefore blessings evermore
    on thee doth God bestow.

³Thy sword gird on thy thigh,
   thou that art most of might:
Appear in dreadful majesty,
   and in thy glory bright.

⁴For meekness, truth, and right,
   ride prosp'rously in state;
And thy right hand shall teach to thee
   things terrible and great.

⁵Thy shafts shall pierce their hearts
   that foes are to the King;
Whereby into subjection
   the people thou shalt bring.

⁶Thy royal seat, O Lord,
   for ever shall remain:
The sceptre of thy kingdom doth
   all righteousness maintain.

⁷Thou lov'st right, and hat'st ill;
   for God, thy God, most high,
Above thy fellows hath with th' oil
   of joy anointed thee.

⁸Of myrrh and spices sweet
   a smell thy garments had,
Out of the iv'ry palaces,
   whereby they made thee glad.

⁹And in thy glorious train
   kings' daughters waiting stand;
And thy fair queen, in Ophir gold,
   doth stand at thy right hand.

¹⁰O daughter, take good heed,
   incline, and give good ear;
Thou must forget thy kindred all,
   and father's house most dear.

¹¹Thy beauty to the King
   shall then delightful be:
And do thou humbly worship him,
   because thy Lord is he.

¹²The daughter then of Tyre
   there with a gift shall be,
And all the wealthy of the land
   shall make their suit to thee.

¹³The daughter of the King
   all glorious is within;
And with embroideries of gold
   her garments wrought have been.

¹⁴She cometh to the King
   in robes with needle wrought;
The virgins that do follow her
   shall unto thee be brought.

¹⁵They shall be brought with joy,
   and mirth on ev'ry side,
Into the palace of the King,
   and there they shall abide.

¹⁶And in thy fathers' stead,
   thy children thou may'st take,
And in all places of the earth
   them noble princes make.

¹⁷I will shew forth thy name
   to generations all:
Therefore the people evermore
   to thee give praises shall.

Psalm 46

To the chief Musician, for the sons of Korah, A Song upon
Alomoth.

8,6,8,6

¹God is our refuge and our strength,
   in straits a present aid;
²Therefore, although the earth remove,
   we will not be afraid:

Though hills amidst the seas be cast;
   ³Though waters roaring make,
And troubled be; yea, though the hills,
   by swelling seas do shake.

⁴A river is, whose streams do glad
   the city of our God;
The holy place, wherein the Lord
   most high hath his abode.

⁵God in the midst of her doth dwell;
   nothing shall her remove:
The Lord to her an helper will,
   and that right early, prove.

⁶The heathen raged tumultuously,
   the kingdoms moved were:
The Lord God uttered his voice,
   the earth did melt for fear.

⁷The Lord of hosts upon our side
   doth constantly remain:
The God of Jacob's our refuge,
   us safely to maintain.

⁸Come, and behold what wondrous works
   have by the Lord been wrought;
Come, see what desolations
   he on the earth hath brought.

⁹Unto the ends of all the earth
   wars into peace he turns:
The bow he breaks, the spear he cuts,
   in fire the chariot burns.

¹⁰Be still, and know that I am God;
   among the heathen I
Will be exalted; I on earth
   will be exalted high.

¹¹Our God, who is the Lord of hosts,
   is still upon our side;
The God of Jacob our refuge
   for ever will abide.

Psalm 47

To the chief Musician, A Psalm for the sons of Korah.

8,6,8,6

1All people, clap your hands; to God
  with voice of triumph shout:
2For dreadful is the Lord most high,
  great King the earth throughout.

3The heathen people under us
  he surely shall subdue;
And he shall make the nations
  under our feet to bow.

4The lot of our inheritance
  choose out for us shall he,
Of Jacob, whom he loved well,
  ev'n the excellency.

5God is with shouts gone up, the Lord
  with trumpets sounding high.
6Sing praise to God, sing praise, sing praise,
  praise to our King sing ye.

7For God is King of all the earth;
  with knowledge praise express.
8God rules the nations: God sits on
  his throne of holiness.

9The princes of the people are
  assembled willingly;
Ev'n of the God of Abraham
  they who the people be.

For why? the shields that do defend
  the earth are only his:
They to the Lord belong; yea, he
  exalted greatly is.

Psalm 48

A Song and Psalm for the sons of Korah.

8,6,8,6

[1]Great is the Lord, and greatly he
   is to be praised still,
Within the city of our God,
   upon his holy hill.

[2]Mount Zion stands most beautiful,
   the joy of all the land;
The city of the mighty King
   on her north side doth stand.

[3]The Lord within her palaces
   is for a refuge known.
[4]For, lo, the kings that gathered were
   together, by have gone.

[5]But when they did behold the same,
   they, wond'ring, would not stay;
But, being troubled at the sight,
   they thence did haste away.

[6]Great terror there took hold on them;
   they were possessed with fear;
Their grief came like a woman's pain,
   when she a child doth bear.

[7]Thou Tarshish ships with east wind break'st:
   [8]As we have heard it told,
So, in the city of the Lord,
   our eyes did it behold;

In our God's city, which his hand
   for ever stablish will.
[9]We of thy loving-kindness thought,
   Lord, in thy temple still.

[10]O Lord, according to thy name,
   through all the earth's thy praise;
And thy right hand, O Lord, is full
   of righteousness always.

[11]Because thy judgments are made known,
   let Zion mount rejoice;
Of Judah let the daughters all
   send forth a cheerful voice.

[12]Walk about Zion, and go round;
   the high tow'rs thereof tell:
[13]Consider ye her palaces,
   and mark her bulwarks well;

That ye may tell posterity.
   [14]For this God doth abide
Our God for evermore; he will
   ev'n unto death us guide.

Psalm 49

To the chief Musician, A Psalm for the sons of Korah.

                                       8,6,8,6

[1]Hear this, all people, and give ear,
   all in the world that dwell;
[2]Both low and high, both rich and poor.
   [3]My mouth shall wisdom tell:

My heart shall knowledge meditate.
   [4]I will incline mine ear
To parables, and on the harp
   my sayings dark declare.

[5]Amidst those days that evil be,
   why should I, fearing, doubt?
When of my heels th' iniquity
   shall compass me about.

[6]Whoe'er they be that in their wealth
   their confidence do pitch,
And boast themselves, because they are
   become exceeding rich:

[7]Yet none of these his brother can
   redeem by any way;
Nor can he unto God for him
   sufficient ransom pay,

8(Their soul's redemption precious is,
   and it can never be,)
9That still he should for ever live,
   and not corruption see.

10For why? he seeth that wise men die,
   and brutish fools also
Do perish; and their wealth, when dead,
   to others they let go.

11Their inward thought is, that their house
   and dwelling-places shall
Stand through all ages; they their lands
   by their own names do call.

12But yet in honour shall not man
   abide continually;
But passing hence, may be compared
   unto the beasts that die.

13Thus brutish folly plainly is
   their wisdom and their way;
Yet their posterity approve
   what they do fondly say.

14Like sheep they in the grave are laid,
   and death shall them devour;
And in the morning upright men
   shall over them have pow'r:

Their beauty from their dwelling shall
   consume within the grave.
15But from hell's hand God will me free,
   for he shall me receive.

16Be thou not then afraid when one
   enriched thou dost see,
Nor when the glory of his house
   advanced is on high:

17For he shall carry nothing hence
   when death his days doth end;
Nor shall his glory after him
   into the grave descend.

18Although he his own soul did bless
    whilst he on earth did live;
(And when thou to thyself dost well,
    men will thee praises give;)

19He to his fathers' race shall go,
    they never shall see light.
20Man honour'd wanting knowledge is
    like beasts that perish quite.

Psalm 50

A Psalm of Asaph.

First Version (S.M.)
6,6,8,6

1The mighty God, the Lord,
    hath spoken, and did call
The earth, from rising of the sun,
    to where he hath his fall.

2From out of Zion hill,
    which of excellency
And beauty the perfection is,
    God shined gloriously.

3Our God shall surely come,
    keep silence shall not he:
Before him fire shall waste, great storms
    shall round about him be.

4Unto the heavens clear
    he from above shall call,
And to the earth likewise, that he
    may judge his people all.

5Together let my saints
    unto me gathered be,
Those that by sacrifice have made
    a covenant with me.

6And then the heavens shall
    his righteousness declare:
Because the Lord himself is he
    by whom men judged are.

⁷My people Isr'el hear,
 speak will I from on high,
Against thee I will testify;
 God, ev'n thy God, am I.

⁸I for thy sacrifice
 no blame will on thee lay,
Nor for burnt-off'rings, which to me
 thou offer'dst ev'ry day.

⁹I'll take no calf nor goats
 from house or fold of thine:
¹⁰For beasts of forests, cattle all
 on thousand hills, are mine.

¹¹The fowls on mountains high
 are all to me well known;
Wild beasts which in the fields do lie,
 ev'n they are all mine own.

¹²Then, if I hungry were,
 I would not tell it thee;
Because the world, and fulness all
 thereof, belongs to me.

¹³Will I eat flesh of bulls?
 or goats' blood drink will I?
¹⁴Thanks offer thou to God, and pay
 thy vows to the most High.

¹⁵And call upon me when
 in trouble thou shalt be;
I will deliver thee, and thou
 my name shalt glorify.

¹⁶But to the wicked man
 God saith, My laws and truth
Should'st thou declare? how dar'st thou take
 my cov'nant in thy mouth?

¹⁷Sith thou instruction hat'st,
 which should thy ways direct;
And sith my words behind thy back
 thou cast'st, and dost reject.

¹⁸When thou a thief didst see,
   with him thou didst consent;
And with the vile adulterers
   partaker on thou went.

¹⁹Thou giv'st thy mouth to ill,
   thy tongue deceit doth frame;
²⁰Thou sitt'st, and 'gainst thy brother speak'st,
   thy mother's son dost shame.

²¹Because I silence kept,
   while thou these things hast wrought;
That I was altogether like
   thyself, hath been thy thought;

Yet I will thee reprove,
   and set before thine eyes,
In order ranked, thy misdeeds
   and thine iniquities.

²²Now, ye that God forget,
   this carefully consider;
Lest I in pieces tear you all,
   and none can you deliver.

²³Whoso doth offer praise
   me glorifies; and I
Will show him God's salvation,
   that orders right his way.

Psalm 50

Second Version (C.M.)
8,6,8,6

¹The mighty God, the Lord, hath spoke,
   and called the earth upon,
Ev'n from the rising of the sun
   unto his going down.

²From out of Zion, his own hill,
   where the perfection high
Of beauty is, from thence the Lord
   hath shined gloriously.

³Our God shall come, and shall no more
 be silent, but speak out:
Before him fire shall waste, great storms
 shall compass him about.

⁴He to the heavens from above,
 and to the earth below,
Shall call, that he his judgments may
 before his people show.

⁵Let all my saints together be
 unto me gathered;
Those that by sacrifice with me
 a covenant have made.

⁶And then the heavens shall declare
 his righteousness abroad:
Because the Lord himself doth come;
 none else is judge but God.

⁷Hear, O my people, and I'll speak;
 O Israel by name,
Against thee I will testify;
 God, ev'n thy God, I am.

⁸I for thy sacrifices few
 reprove thee never will,
Nor for burnt-off'rings to have been
 before me offered still.

⁹I'll take no bullock nor he-goats
 from house nor folds of thine:
¹⁰For beasts of forests, cattle all
 on thousand hills, are mine.

¹¹The fowls are all to me well known
 that mountains high do yield;
And I do challenge as mine own
 the wild beasts of the field.

¹²If I were hungry, I would not
 to thee for need complain;
For earth, and all its fullness, doth
 to me of right pertain.

¹³That I to eat the flesh of bulls
   take pleasure dost thou think?
Or that I need, to quench my thirst,
   the blood of goats to drink?

¹⁴Nay, rather unto me, thy God,
   thanksgiving offer thou:
To the most High perform thy word,
   and fully pay thy vow:

¹⁵And in the day of trouble great
   see that thou call on me;
I will deliver thee, and thou
   my name shalt glorify.

¹⁶But God unto the wicked saith,
   Why should'st thou mention make
Of my commands? how dar'st thou in
   thy mouth my cov'nant take?

¹⁷Sith it is so that thou dost hate
   all good instruction;
And sith thou cast'st behind thy back,
   and slight'st my words each one.

¹⁸When thou a thief didst see, then straight
   thou join'dst with him in sin,
And with the vile adulterers
   thou hast partaker been.

¹⁹Thy mouth to evil thou dost give,
   thy tongue deceit doth frame.
²⁰Thou sitt'st, and 'gainst thy brother speak'st,
   thy mother's son to shame.

²¹These things thou wickedly hast done,
   and I have silent been:
Thou thought'st that I was like thyself,
   and did approve thy sin:

But I will sharply thee reprove,
   and I will order right
Thy sins and thy transgressions
   in presence of thy sight.

²²Consider this, and be afraid,
    ye that forget the Lord,
Lest I in pieces tear you all,
    when none can help afford.

²³Who off'reth praise me glorifies:
    I will show God's salvation
To him that ordereth aright
    his life and conversation.

Psalm 51

To the chief Musician, A Psalm of David, when Nathan
the prophet came unto him, after he had gone into
Bathsheba.

8,6,8,6

¹After thy loving-kindness, Lord,
    have mercy upon me:
For thy compassions great, blot out
    all mine iniquity.

²Me cleanse from sin, and throughly wash
    from mine iniquity:
³For my transgressions I confess;
    my sin I ever see.

⁴'Gainst thee, thee only, have I sinned,
    in thy sight done this ill;
That when thou speak'st thou may'st be just,
    and clear in judging still.

⁵Behold, I in iniquity
    was formed the womb within;
My mother also me conceived
    in guiltiness and sin.

⁶Behold, thou in the inward parts
    with truth delighted art;
And wisdom thou shalt make me know
    within the hidden part.

⁷Do thou with hyssop sprinkle me,
    I shall be cleansed so;
Yea, wash thou me, and then I shall
    be whiter than the snow.

⁸Of gladness and of joyfulness
   make me to hear the voice;
That so these very bones which thou
   hast broken may rejoice.

⁹All mine iniquities blot out,
   thy face hide from my sin.
¹⁰Create a clean heart, Lord, renew
   a right sp'rit me within.

¹¹Cast me not from thy sight, nor take
   thy Holy Sp'rit away.
¹²Restore me thy salvation's joy;
   with thy free Sp'rit me stay.

¹³Then will I teach thy ways unto
   those that transgressors be;
And those that sinners are shall then
   be turned unto thee.

¹⁴O God, of my salvation God,
   me from blood-guiltiness
Set free; then shall my tongue aloud
   sing of thy righteousness.

¹⁵My closed lips, O Lord, by thee
   let them be opened;
Then shall thy praises by my mouth
   abroad be published.

¹⁶For thou desir'st not sacrifice,
   else would I give it thee;
Nor wilt thou with burnt-offering
   at all delighted be.

¹⁷A broken spirit is to God
   a pleasing sacrifice:
A broken and a contrite heart,
   Lord, thou wilt not despise.

¹⁸Show kindness, and do good, O Lord,
   to Zion, thine own hill:
The walls of thy Jerusalem
   build up of thy good will.

¹⁹Then righteous off'rings shall thee please,
    and off'rings burnt, which they
With whole burnt-off'rings, and with calves,
    shall on thine altar lay.

Psalm 52

To the chief Musician, Maschil, A Psalm of David, when
Doeg the Edomite came and told Saul, and said unto him,
David is come to the house of Ahimelech.

                                        8,6,8,6

¹Why dost thou boast, O mighty man,
    of mischief and of ill?
The goodness of Almighty God
    endureth ever still.

²Thy tongue mischievous calumnies
    deviseth subtilely,
Like to a razor sharp to cut,
    working deceitfully.

³Ill more than good, and more than truth
    thou lovest to speak wrong:
⁴Thou lovest all-devouring words,
    O thou deceitful tongue.

⁵So God shall thee destroy for aye,
    remove thee, pluck thee out
Quite from thy house, out of the land
    of life he shall thee root.

⁶The righteous shall it see, and fear,
    and laugh at him they shall:
⁷Lo, this the man is that did not
    make God his strength at all:

But he in his abundant wealth
    his confidence did place;
And he took strength unto himself
    from his own wickedness.

⁸But I am in the house of God
    like to an olive green:
My confidence for ever hath
    upon God's mercy been.

⁹And I for ever will thee praise,
　　because thou hast done this:
I on thy name will wait; for good
　　before thy saints it is.

Psalm 53

To the chief Musician upon Mahalath, Maschil, A Psalm
of David.

8,6,8,6

¹That there is not a God, the fool
　　doth in his heart conclude:
They are corrupt, their works are vile,
　　not one of them doth good.

²The Lord upon the sons of men
　　from heav'n did cast his eyes,
To see if any one there was
　　that sought God, and was wise.

³They altogether filthy are,
　　they all are backward gone;
And there is none that doeth good,
　　no, not so much as one.

⁴These workers of iniquity,
　　do they not know at all,
That they my people eat as bread,
　　and on God do not call?

⁵Ev'n there they were afraid, and stood
　　with trembling, all dismayed,
Whereas there was no cause at all
　　why they should be afraid:

For God his bones that thee besieged
　　hath scattered all abroad;
Thou hast confounded them, for they
　　despised are of God.

⁶Let Isr'el's help from Sion come:
    when back the Lord shall bring
His captives, Jacob shall rejoice,
    and Israel shall sing.

Psalm 54

To the chief Musician on Neginoth, Maschil, A Psalm of
David, when the Ziphims came and said to Saul, Doth
not David hide himself with us?

8,6,8,6

¹Save me, O God, by thy great name,
    and judge me by thy strength:
²My prayer hear, O God; give ear
    unto my words at length.

³For they that strangers are to me
    do up against me rise;
Oppressors seek my soul, and God
    set not before their eyes.

⁴The Lord my God my helper is,
    lo, therefore I am bold:
He taketh part with ev'ry one
    that doth my soul uphold.

⁵Unto mine enemies he shall
    mischief and ill repay:
O for thy truth's sake cut them off,
    and sweep them clean away.

⁶I will a sacrifice to thee
    give with free willingness;
Thy name, O Lord, because 'tis good,
    with praise I will confess.

⁷For he hath me delivered
    from all adversities;
And his desire mine eye hath seen
    upon mine enemies.

Psalm 55

To the chief Musician on Neginoth, Maschil, A Psalm of David.

8,6,8,6

¹Lord, hear my pray'r, hide not thyself
    from my entreating voice:
²Attend and hear me; in my plaint
    I mourn and make a noise.

³Because of th' en'my's voice, and for
    lewd men's oppression great:
On me they cast iniquity,
    and they in wrath me hate.

⁴Sore pained within me is my heart:
    death's terrors on me fall.
⁵On me comes trembling, fear and dread
    o'erwhelmed me withal.

⁶O that I, like a dove, had wings,
    said I, then would I flee
Far hence, that I might find a place
    where I in rest might be.

⁷Lo, then far off I wander would,
    and in the desert stay;
⁸From windy storm and tempest I
    would haste to 'scape away.

⁹O Lord, on them destruction bring,
    and do their tongues divide;
For in the city violence
    and strife I have espied.

¹⁰They day and night upon the walls
    do go about it round:
There mischief is, and sorrow there
    in midst of it is found.

¹¹Abundant wickedness there is
    within her inward part;
And from her streets deceitfulness
    and guile do not depart.

[12]He was no foe that me reproached,
   then that endure I could;
Nor hater that did 'gainst me boast,
   from him me hide I would.

[13]But thou, man, who mine equal, guide,
   and mine acquaintance wast:
[14]We joined sweet counsels, to God's house
   in company we past.

[15]Let death upon them seize, and down
   let them go quick to hell;
For wickedness doth much abound
   among them where they dwell.

[16]I'll call on God: God will me save.
   [17]I'll pray, and make a noise
At ev'ning, morning, and at noon;
   and he shall hear my voice.

[18]He hath my soul delivered,
   that it in peace might be
From battle that against me was;
   for many were with me.

[19]The Lord shall hear, and them afflict,
   of old who hath abode:
Because they never changes have,
   therefore they fear not God.

[20]'Gainst those that were at peace with him
   he hath put forth his hand:
The covenant that he had made,
   by breaking he profaned.

[21]More smooth than butter were his words,
   while in his heart was war;
His speeches were more soft than oil,
   and yet drawn swords they are.

[22]Cast thou thy burden on the Lord,
   and he shall thee sustain;
Yea, he shall cause the righteous man
   unmoved to remain.

²³But thou, O Lord my God, those men
   in justice shalt o'erthrow,
And in destruction's dungeon dark
   at last shalt lay them low:

The bloody and deceitful men
   shall not live half their days:
But upon thee with confidence
   I will depend always.

Psalm 56

To the chief Musician upon Jonath-elem-rechokim, Mich-
tam of David, when the Philistines took him in Gath.

8,6,8,6

¹Show mercy, Lord, to me, for man
   would swallow me outright;
He me oppresseth, while he doth
   against me daily fight.

²They daily would me swallow up
   that hate me spitefully;
For they be many that do fight
   against me, O most High.

³When I'm afraid I'll trust in thee:
   ⁴In God I'll praise his word;
I will not fear what flesh can do,
   my trust is in the Lord.

⁵Each day they wrest my words; their thoughts
   'gainst me are all for ill.
⁶They meet, they lurk, they mark my steps,
   waiting my soul to kill.

⁷But shall they by iniquity
   escape thy judgments so?
O God, with indignation down
   do thou the people throw.

⁸My wand'rings all what they have been
   thou know'st, their number took;
Into thy bottle put my tears:
   are they not in thy book?

9My foes shall, when I cry, turn back;
  I know't, God is for me.
10In God his word I'll praise; his word
  in God shall praised be.

11In God I trust; I will not fear
  what man can do to me.
12Thy vows upon me are, O God:
  I'll render praise to thee.

13Wilt thou not, who from death me saved,
  my feet from falls keep free,
To walk before God in the light
  of those that living be?

Psalm 57

*To the chief Musician, Al-taschith, Michtam of David,
      when he fled from Saul in the cave.*

8,6,8,6

1Be merciful to me, O God;
  thy mercy unto me
Do thou extend; because my soul
  doth put her trust in thee:

Yea, in the shadow of thy wings
  my refuge I will place,
Until these sad calamities
  do wholly overpass.

2My cry I will cause to ascend
  unto the Lord most high;
To God, who doth all things for me
  perform most perfectly.

3From heav'n he shall send down, and me
  from his reproach defend
That would devour me: God his truth
  and mercy forth shall send.

4My soul among fierce lions is,
  I firebrands live among,
Men's sons, whose teeth are spears and darts,
  a sharp sword is their tongue.

⁵Be thou exalted very high
    above the heav'ns, O God;
Let thou thy glory be advanced
    o'er all the earth abroad.

⁶My soul's bowed down; for they a net
    have laid, my steps to snare:
Into the pit which they have digged
    for me, they fallen are.

⁷My heart is fixed, my heart is fixed,
    O God; I'll sing and praise.
⁸My glory wake; wake psalt'ry, harp;
    myself I'll early raise.

⁹I'll praise thee 'mong the people, Lord;
    'mong nations sing will I:
¹⁰For great to heav'n thy mercy is,
    thy truth is to the sky.

¹¹O Lord, exalted be thy name
    above the heav'ns to stand:
Do thou thy glory far advance
    above both sea and land.

Psalm 58

To the chief Musician, Al-taschith, Michtam of David.

8,6,8,6

¹Do ye, O congregation,
    indeed speak righteousness?
O ye that are the sons of men,
    judge ye with uprightness?

²Yea, ev'n within your very hearts
    ye wickedness have done;
And ye the vi'lence of your hands
    do weigh the earth upon.

³The wicked men estranged are,
    ev'n from the very womb;
They, speaking lies, do stray as soon
    as to the world they come.

⁴Unto a serpent's poison like
    their poison doth appear;
Yea, they are like the adder deaf,
    that closely stops her ear;

⁵That so she may not hear the voice
    of one that charm her would,
No, not though he most cunning were,
    and charm most wisely could.

⁶Their teeth, O God, within their mouth
    break thou in pieces small;
The great teeth break thou out, O Lord,
    of these young lions all.

⁷Let them like waters melt away,
    which downward still do flow:
In pieces cut his arrows all,
    when he shall bend his bow.

⁸Like to a snail that melts away,
    let each of them be gone;
Like woman's birth untimely, that
    they never see the sun.

⁹He shall them take away before
    your pots the thorns can find,
Both living, and in fury great,
    as with a stormy wind.

¹⁰The righteous, when he vengeance sees,
    he shall be joyful then;
The righteous one shall wash his feet
    in blood of wicked men.

¹¹So men shall say, The righteous man
    reward shall never miss:
And verily upon the earth
    a God to judge there is.

Psalm 59

To the chief Musician, Al-taschith, Michtam of David;
when Saul sent, and they watched the house to kill him.

8,6,8,6

¹My God, deliver me from those
    that are mine enemies;
And do thou me defend from those
    that up against me rise.

²Do thou deliver me from them
    that work iniquity;
And give me safety from the men
    of bloody cruelty.

³For, lo, they for my soul lay wait:
    the mighty do combine
Against me, Lord; not for my fault,
    nor any sin of mine.

⁴They run, and, without fault in me,
    themselves do ready make:
Awake to meet me with thy help;
    and do thou notice take.

⁵Awake therefore, Lord God of hosts,
    thou God of Israel,
To visit heathen all: spare none
    that wickedly rebel.

⁶At ev'ning they go to and fro;
    they make great noise and sound,
Like to a dog, and often walk
    about the city round.

⁷Behold, they belch out with their mouth,
    and in their lips are swords:
For they do say thus, Who is he
    that now doth hear our words?

⁸But thou, O Lord, shalt laugh at them,
    and all the heathen mock.
⁹While he's in pow'r I'll wait on thee;
    for God is my high rock.

¹⁰He of my mercy that is God
    betimes shall me prevent;
Upon mine en'mies God shall let
    me see mine heart's content.

¹¹Them slay not, lest my folk forget;
    but scatter them abroad
By thy strong pow'r; and bring them down,
    O thou our shield and God.

¹²For their mouth's sin, and for the words
    that from their lips do fly,
Let them be taken in their pride;
    because they curse and lie.

¹³In wrath consume them, them consume,
    that so they may not be:
And that in Jacob God doth rule
    to th' earth's ends let them see.

¹⁴At ev'ning let thou them return,
    making great noise and sound,
Like to a dog, and often walk
    about the city round.

¹⁵And let them wander up and down,
    in seeking food to eat;
And let them grudge when they shall not
    be satisfied with meat.

¹⁶But of thy pow'r I'll sing aloud;
    at morn thy mercy praise:
For thou to me my refuge wast,
    and tow'r, in troublous days.

¹⁷O God, thou art my strength, I will
    sing praises unto thee;
For God is my defence, a God
    of mercy unto me.

Psalm 60

*To the chief Musician upon Shushan-eduth, Michtam of
David, to teach; when he strove with Aram-naharaim,
and with Aram-zobah, when Joab returned and smote of
Edom, in the valley of Salt, twelve thousand.*

8,6,8,6

¹⁰ Lord, thou hast rejected us,
    and scattered us abroad;
Thou justly hast displeased been;
    return to us, O God.

²The earth to tremble thou hast made;
    therein didst breaches make:
Do thou thereof the breaches heal,
    because the land doth shake.

³Unto thy people thou hard things
    hast showed, and on them sent;
And thou hast caused us to drink
    wine of astonishment.

⁴And yet a banner thou hast giv'n
    to them who thee do fear;
That it by them, because of truth,
    displayed may appear.

⁵That thy beloved people may
    delivered be from thrall,
Save with the pow'r of thy right hand,
    and hear me when I call.

⁶God in his holiness hath spoke;
    herein I will take pleasure:
Shechem I will divide, and forth
    will Succoth's valley measure.

⁷Gilead I claim as mine by right;
    Manasseh mine shall be;
Ephraim is of mine head the strength;
    Judah gives laws for me;

⁸Moab's my washing-pot; my shoe
    I'll over Edom throw;

And over Palestina's land
   I will in triumph go.

[9]O who is he will bring me to
   the city fortified?
O who is he that to the land
   of Edom will me guide?

[10]O God, which hadest us cast off,
   this thing wilt thou not do?
Ev'n thou, O God, which didest not
   forth with our armies go?

[11]Help us from trouble; for the help
   is vain which man supplies.
[12]Through God we'll do great acts; he shall
   tread down our enemies.

Psalm 61

To the chief Musician upon Neginoth, A Psalm of David.

8,6,8,6

[1]O God, give ear unto my cry;
   unto my pray'r attend.
[2]From th' utmost corner of the land
   my cry to thee I'll send.

What time my heart is overwhelmed,
   and in perplexity,
Do thou me lead unto the Rock
   that higher is than I.

[3]For thou hast for my refuge been
   a shelter by thy pow'r;
And for defence against my foes
   thou hast been a strong tow'r.

[4]Within thy tabernacle I
   for ever will abide;
And under covert of thy wings
   with confidence me hide.

[5]For thou the vows that I did make,
   O Lord my God, didst hear:

Thou hast giv'n me the heritage
   of those thy name that fear.

6A life prolonged for many days
   thou to the king shalt give;
Like many generations be
   the years which he shall live.

7He in God's presence his abode
   for evermore shall have:
O do thou truth and mercy both
   prepare, that may him save.

8And so will I perpetually
   sing praise unto thy name;
That having made my vows, I may
   each day perform the same.

Psalm 62

To the chief Musician, to Jeduthun, A Psalm of David.

8,6,8,6

1My soul with expectation
   depends on God indeed;
My strength and my salvation doth
   from him alone proceed.

2He only my salvation is,
   and my strong rock is he:
He only is my sure defence;
   much moved I shall not be.

3How long will ye against a man
   plot mischief? ye shall all
Be slain; ye as a tott'ring fence
   shall be, and bowing wall.

4They only plot to cast him down
   from his excellency:
They joy in lies; with mouth they bless,
   but they curse inwardly.

⁵My soul, wait thou with patience
    upon thy God alone;
On him dependeth all my hope
    and expectation.

⁶He only my salvation is,
    and my strong rock is he;
He only is my sure defence:
    I shall not moved be.

⁷In God my glory placed is,
    and my salvation sure;
In God the rock is of my strength,
    my refuge most secure.

⁸Ye people, place your confidence
    in him continually;
Before him pour ye out your heart:
    God is our refuge high.

⁹Surely mean men are vanity,
    and great men are a lie;
In balance laid, they wholly are
    more light than vanity.

¹⁰Trust ye not in oppression,
    in robb'ry be not vain;
On wealth set not your hearts, when as
    increased is your gain.

¹¹God hath it spoken once to me,
    yea, this I heard again,
That power to Almighty God
    alone doth appertain.

¹²Yea, mercy also unto thee
    belongs, O Lord, alone:
For thou according to his work
    rewardest ev'ry one.

Psalm 63

*A Psalm of David, when he was in the wilderness of
Judah.*

8,6,8,6

¹Lord, thee my God, I'll early seek:
    my soul doth thirst for thee;
My flesh longs in a dry parched land,
    wherein no waters be:

²That I thy power may behold,
    and brightness of thy face,
As I have seen thee heretofore
    within thy holy place.

³Since better is thy love than life,
    my lips thee praise shall give.
⁴I in thy name will lift my hands,
    and bless thee while I live.

⁵Ev'n as with marrow and with fat
    my soul shall filled be;
Then shall my mouth with joyful lips
    sing praises unto thee:

⁶When I do thee upon my bed
    remember with delight,
And when on thee I meditate
    in watches of the night.

⁷In shadow of thy wings I'll joy;
    for thou mine help hast been.
⁸My soul thee follows hard; and me
    thy right hand doth sustain.

⁹Who seek my soul to spill shall sink
    down to earth's lowest room.
¹⁰They by the sword shall be cut off,
    and foxes' prey become.

¹¹Yet shall the king in God rejoice,
    and each one glory shall
That swear by him: but stopped shall be
    the mouth of liars all.

Psalm 64

To the chief Musician, A Psalm of David.

8,6,8,6

¹When I to thee my prayer make,
   Lord, to my voice give ear;
My life save from the enemy,
   of whom I stand in fear.

²Me from their secret counsel hide
   who do live wickedly;
From insurrection of those men
   that work iniquity:

³Who do their tongues with malice whet,
   and make them cut like swords;
In whose bent bows are arrows set,
   ev'n sharp and bitter words:

⁴That they may at the perfect man
   in secret aim their shot;
Yea, suddenly they dare at him
   to shoot, and fear it not.

⁵In ill encourage they themselves,
   and their snares close do lay:
Together conference they have;
   Who shall them see? they say.

⁶They have searched out iniquities,
   a perfect search they keep:
Of each of them the inward thought,
   and very heart, is deep.

⁷God shall an arrow shoot at them,
   and wound them suddenly:
⁸So their own tongue shall them confound;
   all who them see shall fly.

⁹And on all men a fear shall fall,
   God's works they shall declare;
For they shall wisely notice take
   what these his doings are.

¹⁰In God the righteous shall rejoice,
    and trust upon his might;
Yea, they shall greatly glory all
    in heart that are upright.

Psalm 65

To the chief Musician, A Psalm and Song of David.

                        8,6,8,6

¹Praise waits for thee in Zion, Lord:
    to thee vows paid shall be.
²O thou that hearer art of pray'r,
    all flesh shall come to thee.

³Iniquities, I must confess,
    prevail against me do:
But as for our transgressions,
    them purge away shalt thou.

⁴Blessed is the man whom thou dost chuse,
    and mak'st approach to thee,
That he within thy courts, O Lord,
    may still a dweller be:

We surely shall be satisfied
    with thy abundant grace,
And with the goodness of thy house,
    ev'n of thy holy place.

⁵O God of our salvation,
    thou, in thy righteousness,
By fearful works unto our pray'rs
    thine answer dost express:

Therefore the ends of all the earth,
    and those afar that be
Upon the sea, their confidence,
    O Lord, will place in thee.

⁶Who, being girt with pow'r, sets fast
    by his great strength the hills.
⁷Who noise of seas, noise of their waves,
    and people's tumult, stills.

8Those in the utmost parts that dwell
   are at thy signs afraid:
Th' outgoings of the morn and ev'n
   by thee are joyful made.

9The earth thou visit'st, wat'ring it;
   thou mak'st it rich to grow
With God's full flood; thou corn prepar'st,
   when thou provid'st it so.

10Her rigs thou wat'rest plenteously,
   her furrows settelest:
With show'rs thou dost her mollify,
   her spring by thee is blessed.

11So thou the year most lib'rally
   dost with thy goodness crown;
And all thy paths abundantly
   on us drop fatness down.

12They drop upon the pastures wide,
   that do in deserts lie;
The little hills on ev'ry side
   rejoice right pleasantly.

13With flocks the pastures clothed be,
   the vales with corn are clad;
And now they shout and sing to thee,
   for thou hast made them glad.

Psalm 66

To the chief Musician, A Song or Psalm.

8,6,8,6

1All lands to God in joyful sounds,
   aloft your voices raise.
2Sing forth the honour of his name,
   and glorious make his praise.

3Say unto God, How terrible
   in all thy works art thou!
Through thy great pow'r thy foes to thee
   shall be constrained to bow.

⁴All on the earth shall worship thee,
    they shall thy praise proclaim
In songs: they shall sing cheerfully
    unto thy holy name.

⁵Come, and the works that God hath wrought
    with admiration see:
In's working to the sons of men
    most terrible is he.

⁶Into dry land the sea he turned,
    and they a passage had;
Ev'n marching through the flood on foot,
    there we in him were glad.

⁷He ruleth ever by his pow'r;
    his eyes the nations see:
O let not the rebellious ones
    lift up themselves on high.

⁸Ye people, bless our God; aloud
    the voice speak of his praise:
⁹Our soul in life who safe preserves,
    our foot from sliding stays.

¹⁰For thou didst prove and try us, Lord,
    as men do silver try;
¹¹Brought'st us into the net, and mad'st
    bands on our loins to lie.

¹²Thou hast caused men ride o'er our heads;
    and though that we did pass
Through fire and water, yet thou brought'st
    us to a wealthy place.

¹³I'll bring burnt off'rings to thy house;
    to thee my vows I'll pay,
¹⁴Which my lips uttered, my mouth spake,
    when trouble on me lay.

¹⁵Burnt-sacrifices of fat rams
    with incense I will bring;
Of bullocks and of goats I will
    present an offering.

¹⁶All that fear God, come, hear, I'll tell
   what he did for my soul.
¹⁷I with my mouth unto him cried,
   my tongue did him extol.

¹⁸If in my heart I sin regard,
   the Lord me will not hear:
¹⁹But surely God me heard, and to
   my prayer's voice gave ear.

²⁰O let the Lord, our gracious God,
   for ever blessed be,
Who turned not my pray'r from him,
   nor yet his grace from me.

Psalm 67

To the chief Musician on Neginoth, A Psalm or Song.

First Version (S.M.)

6,6,8,6

¹Lord, bless and pity us,
   shine on us with thy face:
²That th' earth thy way, and nations all
   may know thy saving grace.

³Let people praise thee, Lord;
   let people all thee praise.
⁴O let the nations be glad,
   in songs their voices raise:

Thou'lt justly people judge,
   on earth rule nations all.
⁵Let people praise thee, Lord; let them
   praise thee, both great and small.

⁶The earth her fruit shall yield,
   our God shall blessing send.
⁷God shall us bless; men shall him fear
   unto earth's utmost end.

Psalm 67

Second Version (C.M.)
8,6,8,6

¹Lord, unto us be merciful,
   do thou us also bless;
And graciously cause shine on us
   the brightness of thy face:

²That so thy way upon the earth
   to all men may be known;
Also among the nations all
   thy saving health be shown.

³O let the people praise thee, Lord;
   let people all thee praise.
⁴O let the nations be glad,
   and sing for joy always:

For rightly thou shalt people judge,
   and nations rule on earth.
⁵Let people praise thee, Lord; let all
   the folk praise thee with mirth.

⁶Then shall the earth yield her increase;
   God, our God, bless us shall.
⁷God shall us bless; and of the earth
   the ends shall fear him all.

Psalm 68

To the chief Musician, A Psalm or Song of David.

8,6,8,6

¹Let God arise, and scattered
   let all his en'mies be;
And let all those that do him hate
   before his presence flee.

²As smoke is driv'n, so drive thou them;
   as fire melts wax away,
Before God's face let wicked men
   so perish and decay.

³But let the righteous be glad:
   let them before God's sight

Be very joyful; yea, let them
   rejoice with all their might.

4To God sing, to his name sing praise;
   extol him with your voice,
That rides on heav'n, by his name Jah,
   before his face rejoice.

5Because the Lord a father is
   unto the fatherless;
God is the widow's judge, within
   his place of holiness.

6God doth the solitary set
   in fam'lies: and from bands
The chained doth free; but rebels do
   inhabit parched lands.

7O God, what time thou didst go forth
   before thy people's face;
And when through the great wilderness
   thy glorious marching was;

8Then at God's presence shook the earth,
   then drops from heaven fell;
This Sinai shook before the Lord,
   the God of Israel.

9O God, thou to thine heritage
   didst send a plenteous rain,
Whereby thou, when it weary was,
   didst it refresh again.

10Thy congregation then did make
   their habitation there:
Of thine own goodness for the poor,
   O God, thou didst prepare.

11The Lord himself did give the word,
   the word abroad did spread;
Great was the company of them
   the same who published.

12Kings of great armies foiled were,
   and forced to flee away;

And women, who remained at home,
   did distribute the prey.

13Though ye have lien among the pots,
   like doves ye shall appear,
Whose wings with silver, and with gold
   whose feathers covered are.

14When there th' Almighty scattered kings,
   like Salmon's snow 'twas white.
15God's hill is like to Bashan hill,
   like Bashan hill for height.

16Why do ye leap, ye mountains high?
   this is the hill where God
Desires to dwell; yea, God in it
   for aye will make abode.

17God's chariots twenty thousand are,
   thousands of angels strong;
In's holy place God is, as in
   mount Sinai, them among.

18Thou hast, O Lord, most glorious,
   ascended up on high;
And in triumph victorious led
   captive captivity:

Thou hast received gifts for men,
   for such as did rebel;
Yea, ev'n for them, that God the Lord
   in midst of them might dwell.

19Bless'd be the Lord, who is to us
   of our salvation God;
Who daily with his benefits
   us plenteously doth load.

20He of salvation is the God,
   who is our God most strong;
And unto God the Lord from death
   the issues do belong.

21But surely God shall wound the head
   of those that are his foes;

The hairy scalp of him that still
 on in his trespass goes.

22God said, My people I will bring
 again from Bashan hill;
Yea, from the sea's devouring depths
 them bring again I will;

23That in the blood of enemies
 thy foot imbrued may be,
And of thy dogs dipped in the same
 the tongues thou mayest see.

24Thy goings they have seen, O God;
 the steps of majesty
Of my God, and my mighty King,
 within the sanctuary.

25Before went singers, players next
 on instruments took way;
And them among the damsels were
 that did on timbrels play.

26Within the congregations
 bless God with one accord:
From Isr'el's fountain do ye bless
 and praise the mighty Lord.

27With their prince, little Benjamin,
 princes and council there
Of Judah were, there Zabulon's
 and Napht'li's princes were.

28Thy God commands thy strength; make strong
 what thou wrought'st for us, Lord.
29For thy house at Jerusalem
 kings shall thee gifts afford.

30The spearmen's host, the multitude
 of bulls, which fiercely look,
Those calves which people have forth sent,
 O Lord our God, rebuke,

Till ev'ry one submit himself,
 and silver pieces bring:

The people that delight in war
  disperse, O God and King.

31Those that be princes great shall then
  come out of Egypt lands;
And Ethiopia to God
  shall soon stretch out her hands.

32O all ye kingdoms of the earth,
  sing praises to this King;
For he is Lord that ruleth all,
  unto him praises sing.

33To him that rides on heav'ns of heav'ns,
  which he of old did found;
Lo, he sends out his voice, a voice
  in might that doth abound.

34Strength unto God do ye ascribe;
  for his excellency
Is over Israel, his strength
  is in the clouds most high.

35Thou'rt from thy temple dreadful, Lord;
  Isr'el's own God is he,
Who gives his people strength and pow'r:
  O let God blessed be.

Psalm 69

*To the chief Musician upon Shoshannim, A Psalm of
David.*

8,6,8,6

1Save me, O God, because the floods
  do so environ me,
That ev'n unto my very soul
  come in the waters be.

2I downward in deep mire do sink,
  where standing there is none:
I am into deep waters come,
  where floods have o'er me gone.

3I weary with my crying am,
  my throat is also dried;

Mine eyes do fail, while for my God
   I waiting do abide.

⁴Those men that do without a cause
   bear hatred unto me,
Than are the hairs upon my head
   in number more they be:

They that would me destroy, and are
   mine en'mies wrongfully,
Are mighty: so what I took not,
   to render forced was I.

⁵Lord, thou my folly know'st, my sins
   not cover'd are from thee.
⁶Let none that wait on thee be sham'd,
   Lord God of hosts, for me.

O Lord, the God of Israel,
   let none, who search do make,
And seek thee, be at any time
   confounded for my sake.

⁷For I have borne reproach for thee,
   my face is hid with shame.
⁸To brethren strange, to mother's sons
   an alien I became.

⁹Because the zeal did eat me up,
   which to thine house I bear;
And the reproaches cast at thee,
   upon me fallen are.

¹⁰My tears and fasts, t' afflict my soul,
   were turned to my shame.
¹¹When sackcloth I did wear, to them
   a proverb I became.

¹²The men that in the gate do sit
   against me evil spake;
They also that vile drunkards were
   of me their song did make.

¹³But, in an acceptable time,
   my pray'r, Lord, is to thee:

In truth of thy salvation, Lord,
    and mercy great, hear me.

14Deliver me out of the mire,
    from sinking do me keep;
Free me from those that do me hate,
    and from the waters deep.

15Let not the flood on me prevail,
    whose water overflows;
Nor deep me swallow, nor the pit
    her mouth upon me close.

16Hear me, O Lord, because thy love
    and kindness is most good;
Turn unto me, according to
    thy mercies' multitude.

17Nor from thy servant hide thy face:
    I'm troubled, soon attend.
18Draw near my soul, and it redeem;
    me from my foes defend.

19To thee is my reproach well known,
    my shame, and my disgrace:
Those that mine adversaries be
    are all before thy face.

20Reproach hath broke my heart; I'm full
    of grief: I looked for one
To pity me, but none I found;
    comforters found I none.

21They also bitter gall did give
    unto me for my meat:
They gave me vinegar to drink,
    when as my thirst was great.

22Before them let their table prove
    a snare; and do thou make
Their welfare and prosperity
    a trap themselves to take.

23Let thou their eyes so darkened be,
    that sight may them forsake;

And let their loins be made by thee
  continually to shake.

24Thy fury pour thou out on them,
  and indignation;
And let thy wrathful anger, Lord,
  fast hold take them upon.

25All waste and desolate let be
  their habitation;
And in their tabernacles all
  inhabitants be none.

26Because him they do persecute,
  whom thou didst smite before;
They talk unto the grief of those
  whom thou hast wounded sore.

27Add thou iniquity unto
  their former wickedness;
And do not let them come at all
  into thy righteousness.

28Out of the book of life let them
  be razed and blotted quite;
Among the just and righteous
  let not their names be writ.

29But now become exceeding poor
  and sorrowful am I:
By thy salvation, O my God,
  let me be set on high.

30The name of God I with a song
  most cheerfully will praise;
And I, in giving thanks to him,
  his name shall highly raise.

31This to the Lord a sacrifice
  more gracious shall prove
Than bullock, ox, or any beast
  that hath both horn and hoof.

32When this the humble men shall see,
  it joy to them shall give:

O all ye that do seek the Lord,
    your hearts shall ever live.

33For God the poor hears, and will not
    his prisoners contemn.
34Let heav'n, and earth, and seas, him praise,
    and all that move in them.

35For God will Judah's cities build,
    and he will Zion save,
That they may dwell therein, and it
    in sure possession have.

36And they that are his servants' seed
    inherit shall the same;
So shall they have their dwelling there
    that love his blessed name.

Psalm 70

To the chief Musician, A Psalm of David, to bring to
remembrance.

First Version (S.M.)
6,6,8,6

1Lord, haste me to deliver;
    with speed, Lord, succour me.
2Let them that for my soul do seek
    shamed and confounded be:

Turned back be they, and shamed,
    that in my hurt delight.
3Turned back be they, Ha, ha! that say,
    their shaming to requite.

4In thee let all be glad,
    and joy that seek for thee:
Let them who thy salvation love
    say still, God praised be.

5I poor and needy am;
    come, Lord, and make no stay:
My help thou and deliv'rer art;
    O Lord, make no delay.

Psalm 70

Second Version (C.M.)
8,6,8,6

¹Make haste, O God, me to preserve;
   with speed, Lord, succour me.
²Let them that for my soul do seek
   shamed and confounded be:

Let them be turned back, and shamed,
   that in my hurt delight.
³Turned back be they, Ha, ha! that say,
   their shaming to requite.

⁴O Lord, in thee let all be glad,
   and joy that seek for thee:
Let them who thy salvation love
   say still, God praised be.

⁵But I both poor and needy am;
   come, Lord, and make no stay:
My help thou and deliv'rer art;
   O Lord, make no delay.

Psalm 71

8,6,8,6

¹O Lord, my hope and confidence
   is placed in thee alone;
Then let thy servant never be
   put to confusion.

²And let me, in thy righteousness,
   from thee deliv'rance have;
Cause me escape, incline thine ear
   unto me, and me save.

³Be thou my dwelling-rock, to which
   I ever may resort:
Thou gav'st commandment me to save,
   for thou'rt my rock and fort.

⁴Free me, my God, from wicked hands,
   hands cruel and unjust:
⁵For thou, O Lord God, art my hope,
   and from my youth my trust.

⁶Thou from the womb didst hold me up;
   thou art the same that me
Out of my mother's bowels took;
   I ever will praise thee.

⁷To many I a wonder am;
   but thou'rt my refuge strong.
⁸Filled let my mouth be with thy praise
   and honour all day long.

⁹O do not cast me off, when as
   old age doth overtake me;
And when my strength decayed is,
   then do not thou forsake me.

¹⁰For those that are mine enemies
   against me speak with hate;
And they together counsel take
   that for my soul lay wait.

¹¹They said, God leaves him; him pursue
   and take: none will him save.
¹²Be thou not far from me, my God:
   thy speedy help I crave.

¹³Confound, consume them, that unto
   my soul are enemies:
Clothed be they with reproach and shame
   that do my hurt devise.

¹⁴But I with expectation
   will hope continually;
And yet with praises more and more
   I will thee magnify.

¹⁵Thy justice and salvation
   my mouth abroad shall show,
Ev'n all the day; for I thereof
   the numbers do not know.

¹⁶And I will constantly go on
   in strength of God the Lord;
And thine own righteousness, ev'n thine
   alone, I will record.

¹⁷For even from my youth, O God,
   by thee I have been taught;
And hitherto I have declar'd
   the wonders thou hast wrought.

¹⁸And now, Lord, leave me not, when I
   old and gray-headed grow:
Till to this age thy strength and pow'r
   to all to come I show.

¹⁹And thy most perfect righteousness
   O Lord, is very high,
Who hast so great things done: O God,
   who is like unto thee?

²⁰Thou, Lord, who great adversities,
   and sore, to me didst show,
Shalt quicken, and bring me again
   from depths of earth below.

²¹My greatness and my pow'r thou wilt
   increase, and far extend:
On ev'ry side against all grief
   thou wilt me comfort send.

²²Thee, ev'n thy truth, I'll also praise,
   my God, with psaltery:
Thou Holy One of Israel,
   with harp I'll sing to thee.

²³My lips shall much rejoice in thee,
   when I thy praises sound;
My soul, which thou redeemed hast,
   in joy shall much abound.

²⁴My tongue thy justice shall proclaim,
   continuing all day long;
For they confounded are, and shamed,
   that seek to do me wrong.

Psalm 72

A Psalm for Solomon.

8,6,8,6

¹O Lord, thy judgments give the king,
  his son thy righteousness.
²With right he shall thy people judge,
  thy poor with uprightness.

³The lofty mountains shall bring forth
  unto the people peace;
Likewise the little hills the same
  shall do by righteousness.

⁴The people's poor ones he shall judge,
  the needy's children save;
And those shall he in pieces break
  who them oppressed have.

⁵They shall thee fear, while sun and moon
  do last, through ages all.
⁶Like rain on mown grass he shall drop,
  or show'rs on earth that fall.

⁷The just shall flourish in his days,
  and prosper in his reign:
He shall, while doth the moon endure,
  abundant peace maintain.

⁸His large and great dominion shall
  from sea to sea extend:
It from the river shall reach forth
  unto earth's utmost end.

⁹They in the wilderness that dwell
  bow down before him must;
And they that are his enemies
  shall lick the very dust.

¹⁰The kings of Tarshish, and the isles,
  to him shall presents bring;
And unto him shall offer gifts
  Sheba's and Seba's king.

[11]Yea, all the mighty kings on earth
    before him down shall fall;
And all the nations of the world
    do service to him shall.

[12]For he the needy shall preserve,
    when he to him doth call;
The poor also, and him that hath
    no help of man at all.

[13]The poor man and the indigent
    in mercy he shall spare;
He shall preserve alive the souls
    of those that needy are.

[14]Both from deceit and violence
    their soul he shall set free;
And in his sight right precious
    and dear their blood shall be.

[15]Yea, he shall live, and giv'n to him
    shall be of Sheba's gold:
For him still shall they pray, and he
    shall daily be extolled.

[16]Of corn an handful in the earth
    on tops of mountains high,
With prosp'rous fruit shall shake, like trees
    on Lebanon that be.

The city shall be flourishing,
    her citizens abound
In number shall, like to the grass
    that grows upon the ground.

[17]His name for ever shall endure;
    last like the sun it shall:
Men shall be blessed in him, and blessed
    all nations shall him call.

[18]Now blessed be the Lord our God,
    the God of Israel,
For he alone doth wondrous works,
    in glory that excel.

¹⁹And blessed be his glorious name
     to all eternity:
The whole earth let his glory fill.
     Amen, so let it be.

Psalm 73

A Psalm of Asaph.

8,6,8,6

¹Yet God is good to Israel,
     to each pure-hearted one.
²But as for me, my steps near slipped,
     my feet were almost gone.

³For I envious was, and grudged
     the foolish folk to see,
When I perceived the wicked sort
     enjoy prosperity.

⁴For still their strength continueth firm;
     their death of bands is free.
⁵They are not toiled like other men,
     nor plagued, as others be.

⁶Therefore their pride, like to a chain,
     them compasseth about;
And, as a garment, violence
     doth cover them throughout.

⁷Their eyes stand out with fat; they have
     more than their hearts could wish.
⁸They are corrupt; their talk of wrong
     both lewd and lofty is.

⁹They set their mouth against the heav'ns
     in their blasphemous talk;
And their reproaching tongue throughout
     the earth at large doth walk.

¹⁰His people oftentimes for this
     look back, and turn about;
Sith waters of so full a cup
     to these are poured out.

¹¹And thus they say, How can it be
    that God these things doth know?
Or, Can there in the Highest be
    knowledge of things below?

¹²Behold, these are the wicked ones,
    yet prosper at their will
In worldly things; they do increase
    in wealth and riches still.

¹³I verily have done in vain
    my heart to purify;
To no effect in innocence
    washed my hands have I.

¹⁴For daily, and all day throughout,
    great plagues I suffered have;
Yea, ev'ry morning I of new
    did chastisement receive.

¹⁵If in this manner foolishly
    to speak I would intend,
Thy children's generation,
    behold, I should offend.

¹⁶When I this thought to know, it was
    too hard a thing for me;
¹⁷Till to God's sanctuary I went,
    then I their end did see.

¹⁸Assuredly thou didst them set
    a slipp'ry place upon;
Them suddenly thou castedst down
    into destruction.

¹⁹How in a moment suddenly
    to ruin brought are they!
With fearful terrors utterly
    they are consumed away.

²⁰Ev'n like unto a dream, when one
    from sleeping doth arise;
So thou, O Lord, when thou awak'st,
    their image shalt despise.

²¹Thus grieved was my heart in me,
and me my reins oppressed:
²²So rude was I, and ignorant,
and in thy sight a beast.

²³Nevertheless continually,
O Lord, I am with thee:
Thou dost me hold by my right hand,
and still upholdest me.

²⁴Thou, with thy counsel, while I live,
wilt me conduct and guide;
And to thy glory afterward
receive me to abide.

²⁵Whom have I in the heavens high
but thee, O Lord, alone?
And in the earth whom I desire
besides thee there is none.

²⁶My flesh and heart doth faint and fail,
but God doth fail me never:
For of my heart God is the strength
and portion for ever.

²⁷For, lo, they that are far from thee
for ever perish shall;
Them that a whoring from thee go
thou hast destroyed all.

²⁸But surely it is good for me
that I draw near to God:
In God I trust, that all thy works
I may declare abroad.

Psalm 74

Maschil of Asaph.

8,6,8,6

¹O God, why hast thou cast us off?
is it for evermore?
Against thy pasture-sheep why doth
thine anger smoke so sore?

²O call to thy rememberance
    thy congregation,
Which thou hast purchased of old;
    still think the same upon:

The rod of thine inheritance,
    which thou redeemed hast,
This Zion hill, wherein thou hadst
    thy dwelling in times past.

³To these long desolations
    thy feet lift, do not tarry;
For all the ills thy foes have done
    within thy sanctuary.

⁴Amidst thy congregations
    thine enemies do roar:
Their ensigns they set up for signs
    of triumph thee before.

⁵A man was famous, and was had
    in estimation,
According as he lifted up
    his axe thick trees upon.

⁶But all at once with axes now
    and hammers they go to,
And down the carved work thereof
    they break, and quite undo.

⁷They fired have thy sanctuary,
    and have defiled the same,
By casting down unto the ground
    the place where dwelt thy name.

⁸Thus said they in their hearts, Let us
    destroy them out of hand:
They burnt up all the synagogues
    of God within the land.

⁹Our signs we do not now behold;
    there is not us among
A prophet more, nor any one
    that knows the time how long.

¹⁰How long, Lord, shall the enemy
    thus in reproach exclaim?
And shall the adversary thus
    always blaspheme thy name?

¹¹Thy hand, ev'n thy right hand of might,
    why dost thou thus draw back?
O from thy bosom pluck it out
    for our deliv'rance sake.

¹²For certainly God is my King,
    ev'n from the times of old,
Working in midst of all the earth
    salvation manifold.

¹³The sea, by thy great pow'r, to part
    asunder thou didst make;
And thou the dragons' heads, O Lord,
    within the waters brake.

¹⁴The leviathan's head thou brak'st
    in pieces, and didst give
Him to be meat unto the folk
    in wilderness that live.

¹⁵Thou clav'st the fountain and the flood,
    which did with streams abound:
Thou dry'dst the mighty waters up
    unto the very ground.

¹⁶Thine only is the day, O Lord,
    thine also is the night;
And thou alone prepared hast
    the sun and shining light.

¹⁷By thee the borders of the earth
    were settled ev'ry where:
The summer and the winter both
    by thee created were.

¹⁸That th' enemy reproached hath,
    O keep it in record;
And that the foolish people have
    blasphemed thy name, O Lord.

[19]Unto the multitude do not
    thy turtle's soul deliver:
The congregation of thy poor
    do not forget for ever.

[20]Unto thy cov'nant have respect;
    for earth's dark places be
Full of the habitations
    of horrid cruelty.

[21]O let not those that be oppressed
    return again with shame:
Let those that poor and needy are
    give praise unto thy name.

[22]Do thou, O God, arise and plead
    the cause that is thine own:
Remember how thou art reproached
    still by the foolish one.

[23]Do not forget the voice of those
    that are thine enemies:
Of those the tumult ever grows
    that do against thee rise.

Psalm 75

To the chief Musician, Al-taschith, A Psalm or Song of
Asaph.

8,6,8,6

[1]To thee, O God, do we give thanks,
    we do give thanks to thee;
Because thy wondrous works declare
    thy great name near to be.

[2]I purpose, when I shall receive
    the congregation,
That I shall judgment uprightly
    render to ev'ry one.

[3]Dissolved is the land, with all
    that in the same do dwell;
But I the pillars thereof do
    bear up, and stablish well.

⁴I to the foolish people said,
  Do not deal foolishly;
And unto those that wicked are,
  Lift not your horn on high.

⁵Lift not your horn on high, nor speak
  ⁶with stubborn neck. But know,
That not from east, nor west, nor south,
  promotion doth flow.

⁷But God is judge; he puts down one,
  and sets another up.
⁸For in the hand of God most high
  of red wine is a cup:

'Tis full of mixture, he pours forth,
  and makes the wicked all
Wring out the bitter dregs thereof;
  yea, and they drink them shall.

⁹But I for ever will declare,
  I Jacob's God will praise.
¹⁰All horns of lewd men I'll cut off;
  but just men's horns will raise.

Psalm 76

*To the chief Musician on Neginoth, A Psalm or Song of
Asaph.*

8,6,8,6

¹In Judah's land God is well known,
  his name's in Isr'el great:
²In Salem is his tabernacle,
  in Zion is his seat.

³There arrows of the bow he brake,
  the shield, the sword, the war.
⁴More glorious thou than hills of prey,
  more excellent art far.

⁵Those that were stout of heart are spoiled,
  they slept their sleep outright;
And none of those their hands did find,
  that were the men of might.

⁶When thy rebuke, O Jacob's God,
    had forth against them past,
Their horses and their chariots both
    were in a dead sleep cast.

⁷Thou, Lord, ev'n thou art he that should
    be feared; and who is he
That may stand up before thy sight,
    if once thou angry be?

⁸From heav'n thou judgment caused be heard;
    the earth was still with fear,
⁹When God to judgment rose, to save
    all meek on earth that were.

¹⁰Surely the very wrath of man
    unto thy praise redounds:
Thou to the remnant of his wrath
    wilt set restraining bounds.

¹¹Vow to the Lord your God, and pay:
    all ye that near him be,
Bring gifts and presents unto him;
    for to be feared is he.

¹²By him the sp'rits shall be cut off
    of those that princes are:
Unto the kings that are on earth
    he fearful doth appear.

Psalm 77

To the chief Musician, to Jeduthun, A Psalm of Asaph.

8,6,8,6

¹Unto the Lord I with my voice,
    I unto God did cry;
Ev'n with my voice, and unto me
    his ear he did apply.

²I in my trouble sought the Lord,
    my sore by night did run,
And ceased not; my grieved soul
    did consolation shun.

³I to remembrance God did call,
    yet trouble did remain;
And overwhelmed my spirit was,
    whilst I did sore complain.

⁴Mine eyes, debarred from rest and sleep,
    thou makest still to wake;
My trouble is so great that I
    unable am to speak.

⁵The days of old to mind I called,
    and oft did think upon
The times and ages that are past
    full many years agone.

⁶By night my song I call to mind,
    and commune with my heart;
My sp'rit did carefully enquire
    how I might ease my smart.

⁷For ever will the Lord cast off,
    and gracious be no more?
⁸For ever is his mercy gone?
    fails his word evermore?

⁹Is't true that to be gracious
    the Lord forgotten hath?
And that his tender mercies he
    hath shut up in his wrath?

¹⁰Then did I say, That surely this
    is mine infirmity:
I'll mind the years of the right hand
    of him that is most High.

¹¹Yea, I remember will the works
    performed by the Lord:
The wonders done of old by thee
    I surely will record.

¹²I also will of all thy works
    my meditation make;
And of thy doings to discourse
    great pleasure I will take.

[13]O God, thy way most holy is
    within thy sanctuary;
And what god is so great in pow'r
    as is our God most high?

[14]Thou art the God that wonders do'st
    by thy right hand most strong:
Thy mighty pow'r thou hast declared
    the nations among.

[15]To thine own people with thine arm
    thou didst redemption bring;
To Jacob's sons, and to the tribes
    of Joseph that do spring.

[16]The waters, Lord, perceived thee,
    the waters saw thee well;
And they for fear aside did flee;
    the depths on trembling fell.

[17]The clouds in water forth were poured,
    sound loudly did the sky;
And swiftly through the world abroad
    thine arrows fierce did fly.

[18]Thy thunder's voice alongst the heav'n
    a mighty noise did make;
By lightnings lightened was the world,
    th' earth tremble did and shake.

[19]Thy way is in the sea, and in
    the waters great thy path;
Yet are thy footsteps hid, O Lord;
    none knowledge thereof hath.

[20]Thy people thou didst safely lead,
    like to a flock of sheep;
By Moses' hand and Aaron's thou
    didst them conduct and keep.

Psalm 78

Maschil of Asaph.

8,6,8,6

¹Attend, my people, to my law;
　　thereto give thou an ear;
The words that from my mouth proceed
　　attentively do hear.

²My mouth shall speak a parable,
　　and sayings dark of old;
³The same which we have heard and known,
　　and us our fathers told.

⁴We also will them not conceal
　　from their posterity;
Them to the generation
　　to come declare will we:

The praises of the Lord our God,
　　and his almighty strength,
The wondrous works that he hath done,
　　we will show forth at length.

⁵His testimony and his law
　　in Isr'el he did place,
And charged our fathers it to show
　　to their succeeding race;

⁶That so the race which was to come
　　might well them learn and know;
And sons unborn, who should arise,
　　might to their sons them show:

⁷That they might set their hope in God,
　　and suffer not to fall
His mighty works out of their mind,
　　but keep his precepts all:

⁸And might not, like their fathers, be
　　a stiff rebellious race;
A race not right in heart; with God
　　whose sp'rit not steadfast was.

⁹The sons of Ephraim, who nor bows
    nor other arms did lack,
When as the day of battle was,
    they faintly turned back.

¹⁰They brake God's cov'nant, and refused
    in his commands to go;
¹¹His works and wonders they forgot,
    which he to them did show.

¹²Things marvellous he brought to pass;
    their fathers them beheld
Within the land of Egypt done,
    yea, ev'n in Zoan's field.

¹³By him divided was the sea,
    he caused them through to pass;
And made the waters so to stand,
    as like an heap it was.

¹⁴With cloud by day, with light of fire
    all night, he did them guide.
¹⁵In desert rocks he clave, and drink,
    as from great depths, supplied.

¹⁶He from the rock brought streams, like floods
    made waters to run down.
¹⁷Yet sinning more, in desert they
    provoked the Highest One.

¹⁸For in their heart they tempted God,
    and, speaking with mistrust,
They greedily did meat require
    to satisfy their lust.

¹⁹Against the Lord himself they spake,
    and, murmuring, said thus,
A table in the wilderness
    can God prepare for us?

²⁰Behold, he smote the rock, and thence
    came streams and waters great;
But can he give his people bread?
    and send them flesh to eat?

21The Lord did hear, and waxed wroth;
    so kindled was a flame
'Gainst Jacob, and 'gainst Israel
    up indignation came.

22For they believed not God, nor trust
    in his salvation had;
23Though clouds above he did command,
    and heav'n's doors open made,

24And manna rained on them, and gave
    them corn of heav'n to eat.
25Man angels' food did eat; to them
    he to the full sent meat.

26And in the heaven he did cause
    an eastern wind to blow;
And by his power he let out
    the southern wind to go.

27Then flesh as thick as dust he made
    to rain down them among;
And feathered fowls, like as the sand
    which li'th the shore along.

28At his command amidst their camp
    these show'rs of flesh down fell,
All round about the tabernacles
    and tents where they did dwell.

29So they did eat abundantly,
    and had of meat their fill;
For he did give to them what was
    their own desire and will.

30They from their lust had not estranged
    their heart and their desire;
But while the meat was in their mouths,
    which they did so require,

31God's wrath upon them came, and slew
    the fattest of them all;
So that the choice of Israel,
    o'erthrown by death, did fall.

³²Yet, notwithstanding of all this,
   they sinned still the more;
And though he had great wonders wrought,
   believed him not therefore:

³³Wherefore their days in vanity
   he did consume and waste;
And by his wrath their wretched years
   away in trouble past.

³⁴But when he slew them, then they did
   to seek him show desire;
Yea, they returned, and after God
   right early did enquire.

³⁵And that the Lord had been their Rock,
   they did remember then;
Ev'n that the high almighty God
   had their Redeemer been.

³⁶Yet with their mouth they flattered him,
   and spake but feignedly;
And they unto the God of truth
   with their false tongues did lie.

³⁷For though their words were good, their heart
   with him was not sincere;
Unsteadfast and perfidious
   they in his cov'nant were.

³⁸But, full of pity, he forgave
   their sin, them did not slay;
Nor stirred up all his wrath, but oft
   his anger turned away.

³⁹For that they were but fading flesh
   to mind he did recall;
A wind that passeth soon away,
   and not returns at all.

⁴⁰How often did they him provoke
   within the wilderness!
And in the desert did him grieve
   with their rebelliousness!

⁴¹Yea, turning back, they tempted God,
    and limits set upon
Him, who in midst of Isr'el is
    the only Holy One.

⁴²They did not call to mind his pow'r,
    nor yet the day when he
Delivered them out of the hand
    of their fierce enemy;

⁴³Nor how great signs in Egypt land
    he openly had wrought;
What miracles in Zoan's field
    his hand to pass had brought.

⁴⁴How lakes and rivers ev'ry where
    he turned into blood;
So that nor man nor beast could drink
    of standing lake or flood.

⁴⁵He brought among them swarms of flies,
    which did them sore annoy;
And diverse kinds of filthy frogs
    he sent them to destroy.

⁴⁶He to the caterpillar gave
    the fruits of all their soil;
Their labours he delivered up
    unto the locusts' spoil.

⁴⁷Their vines with hail, their sycamores
    he with the frost did blast:
⁴⁸Their beasts to hail he gave; their flocks
    hot thunderbolts did waste.

⁴⁹Fierce burning wrath he on them cast,
    and indignation strong,
And troubles sore, by sending forth
    ill angels them among.

⁵⁰He to his wrath made way; their soul
    from death he did not save;
But over to the pestilence
    the lives of them he gave.

[51]In Egypt land the first-born all
　　he smote down ev'ry where;
Among the tents of Ham, ev'n these
　　chief of their strength that were.

[52]But his own people, like to sheep,
　　thence to go forth he made;
And he, amidst the wilderness,
　　them, as a flock, did lead.

[53]And he them safely on did lead,
　　so that they did not fear;
Whereas their en'mies by the sea
　　quite overwhelmed were.

[54]To borders of his sanctuary
　　the Lord his people led,
Ev'n to the mount which his right hand
　　for them had purchased.

[55]The nations of Canaan,
　　by his almighty hand,
Before their face he did expel
　　out of their native land;

Which for inheritance to them
　　by line he did divide,
And made the tribes of Israel
　　within their tents abide.

[56]Yet God most high they did provoke,
　　and tempted ever still;
And to observe his testimonies
　　did not incline their will:

[57]But, like their fathers, turned back,
　　and dealt unfaithfully:
Aside they turned, like a bow
　　that shoots deceitfully.

[58]For they to anger did provoke
　　him with their places high;
And with their graven images
　　moved him to jealousy.

59When God heard this, he waxed wroth,
     and much loathed Isr'el then:
60So Shiloh's tent he left, the tent
     which he had placed with men.

61And he his strength delivered
     into captivity;
He left his glory in the hand
     of his proud enemy.

62His people also he gave o'er
     unto the sword's fierce rage:
So sore his wrath inflamed was
     against his heritage.

63The fire consumed their choice young men;
     their maids no marriage had;
64And when their priests fell by the sword,
     their wives no mourning made.

65But then the Lord arose, as one
     that doth from sleep awake;
And like a giant that, by wine
     refreshed, a shout doth make:

66Upon his en'mies' hinder parts
     he made his stroke to fall;
And so upon them he did put
     a shame perpetual.

67Moreover, he the tabernacle
     of Joseph did refuse;
The mighty tribe of Ephraim
     he would in no wise choose:

68But he did choose Jehudah's tribe
     to be the rest above;
And of mount Zion he made choice,
     which he so much did love.

69And he his sanctuary built
     like to a palace high,
Like to the earth which he did found
     to perpetuity.

⁷⁰Of David, that his servant was,
    he also choice did make,
And even from the folds of sheep
    was pleased him to take:

⁷¹From waiting on the ewes with young,
    he brought him forth to feed
Israel, his inheritance,
    his people, Jacob's seed.

⁷²So after the integrity
    he of his heart them fed;
And by the good skill of his hands
    them wisely governed.

Psalm 79

A Psalm of Asaph.

8,6,8,6

¹O God, the heathen entered have
    thine heritage; by them
Defiled is thy house: on heaps
    they laid Jerusalem.

²The bodies of thy servants they
    have cast forth to be meat
To rav'nous fowls; thy dear saints' flesh
    they gave to beasts to eat.

³Their blood about Jerusalem
    like water they have shed;
And there was none to bury them
    when they were slain and dead.

⁴Unto our neighbours a reproach
    most base become are we;
A scorn and laughingstock to them
    that round about us be.

⁵How long, Lord, shall thine anger last?
    wilt thou still keep the same?
And shall thy fervent jealousy
    burn like unto a flame?

⁶On heathen pour thy fury forth,
    that have thee never known,
And on those kingdoms which thy name
    have never called upon.

⁷For these are they who Jacob have
    devoured cruelly;
And they his habitation
    have caused waste to lie.

⁸Against us mind not former sins;
    thy tender mercies show;
Let them prevent us speedily,
    for we're brought very low.

⁹For thy name's glory help us, Lord,
    who hast our Saviour been:
Deliver us; for thy name's sake,
    O purge away our sin.

¹⁰Why say the heathen, Where's their God?
    let him to them be known;
When those who shed thy servants' blood
    are in our sight o'erthrown.

¹¹O let the pris'ner's sighs ascend
    before thy sight on high;
Preserve those in thy mighty pow'r
    that are designed to die.

¹²And to our neighbours' bosom cause
    it sev'n-fold rendered be,
Ev'n the reproach wherewith they have,
    O Lord, reproached thee.

¹³So we thy folk, and pasture-sheep,
    shall give thee thanks always;
And unto generations all
    we will show forth thy praise.

Psalm 80

To the chief musician upon Shoshannim, Eduth, A Psalm of Asaph.

8,6,8,6

¹Hear, Isr'el's Shepherd! like a flock
   thou that dost Joseph guide;
Shine forth, O thou that dost between
   the cherubims abide.

²In Ephraim's, and Benjamin's
   and in Manasseh's sight,
O come for our salvation;
   stir up thy strength and might.

³Turn us again, O Lord our God,
   and upon us vouchsafe
To make thy countenance to shine,
   and so we shall be safe.

⁴O Lord of hosts, almighty God,
   how long shall kindled be
Thy wrath against the prayer made
   by thine own folk to thee?

⁵Thou tears of sorrow giv'st to them
   instead of bread to eat;
Yea, tears instead of drink thou giv'st
   to them in measure great.

⁶Thou makest us a strife unto
   our neighbours round about;
Our enemies among themselves
   at us do laugh and flout.

⁷Turn us again, O God of hosts,
   and upon us vouchsafe
To make thy countenance to shine,
   and so we shall be safe.

⁸A vine from Egypt brought thou hast,
   by thine outstretched hand;
And thou the heathen out didst cast,
   to plant it in their land.

[9]Before it thou a room didst make,
 where it might grow and stand;
Thou causedst it deep root to take,
 and it did fill the land.

[10]The mountains vailed were with its shade,
 as with a covering;
Like goodly cedars were the boughs
 which out from it did spring.

[11]Upon the one hand to the sea
 her boughs she did out send;
On th' other side unto the flood
 her branches did extend.

[12]Why hast thou then thus broken down,
 and ta'en her hedge away?
So that all passengers do pluck,
 and make of her a prey.

[13]The boar who from the forest comes
 doth waste it at his pleasure;
The wild beast of the field also
 devours it out of measure.

[14]O God of hosts, we thee beseech,
 return now unto thine;
Look down from heav'n in love, behold,
 and visit this thy vine:

[15]This vineyard, which thine own right hand
 hath planted us among;
And that same branch, which for thyself
 thou hast made to be strong.

[16]Burnt up it is with flaming fire,
 it also is cut down:
They utterly are perished,
 when as thy face doth frown.

[17]O let thy hand be still upon
 the Man of thy right hand,
The Son of man, whom for thyself
 thou madest strong to stand.

¹⁸So henceforth we will not go back,
  nor turn from thee at all:
O do thou quicken us, and we
  upon thy name will call.

¹⁹Turn us again, Lord God of hosts,
  and upon us vouchsafe
To make thy countenance to shine,
  and so we shall be safe.

Psalm 81

To the chief Musician upon Gittith, A Psalm of Asaph.

8,6,8,6

¹Sing loud to God our strength; with joy
  to Jacob's God do sing.
²Take up a psalm, the pleasant harp,
  timbrel and psalt'ry bring.

³Blow trumpets at new-moon, what day
  our feast appointed is:
⁴For charge to Isr'el, and a law
  of Jacob's God was this.

⁵To Joseph this a testimony
  he made, when Egypt land
He travelled through, where speech I heard
  I did not understand.

⁶His shoulder I from burdens took,
  his hands from pots did free.
⁷Thou didst in trouble on me call,
  and I delivered thee:

In secret place of thundering
  I did thee answer make;
And at the streams of Meribah
  of thee a proof did take.

⁸O thou, my people, give an ear,
  I'll testify to thee;
To thee, O Isr'el, if thou wilt
  but hearken unto me.

⁹In midst of thee there shall not be
   any strange god at all;
Nor unto any god unknown
   thou bowing down shalt fall.

¹⁰I am the Lord thy God, which did
   from Egypt land thee guide;
I'll fill thy mouth abundantly,
   do thou it open wide.

¹¹But yet my people to my voice
   would not attentive be;
And ev'n my chosen Israel
   he would have none of me.

¹²So to the lust of their own hearts
   I them delivered;
And then in counsels of their own
   they vainly wandered.

¹³O that my people had me heard,
   Isr'el my ways had chose!
¹⁴I had their en'mies soon subdued,
   my hand turned on their foes.

¹⁵The haters of the Lord to him
   submission should have feigned;
But as for them, their time should have
   for evermore remained.

¹⁶He should have also fed them with
   the finest of the wheat;
Of honey from the rock thy fill
   I should have made thee eat.

Psalm 82

A Psalm of Asaph.

8,6,8,6

¹In gods' assembly God doth stand;
   he judgeth gods among.
²How long, accepting persons vile,
   will ye give judgment wrong?

³Defend the poor and fatherless;
    to poor oppressed do right.
⁴The poor and needy ones set free;
    rid them from ill men's might.

⁵They know not, nor will understand;
    in darkness they walk on:
All the foundations of the earth
    out of their course are gone.

⁶I said that ye are gods, and are
    sons of the Highest all:
⁷But ye shall die like men, and as
    one of the princes fall.

⁸O God, do thou raise up thyself,
    the earth to judgment call:
For thou, as thine inheritance,
    shalt take the nations all.

Psalm 83

A Song or Psalm of Asaph.

8,6,8,6

¹Keep not, O God, we thee entreat,
    O keep not silence now:
Do thou not hold thy peace, O God,
    and still no more be thou.

²For, lo, thine enemies a noise
    tumultuously have made;
And they that haters are of thee
    have lifted up the head.

³Against thy chosen people they
    do crafty counsel take;
And they against thy hidden ones
    do consultations make.

⁴Come, let us cut them off, said they,
    from being a nation,
That of the name of Isr'el may
    no more be mention.

⁵For with joint heart they plot, in league
 against thee they combine.
⁶The tents of Edom, Ishm'elites,
 Moab's and Hagar's line;

⁷Gebal, and Ammon, Amalek,
 Philistines, those of Tyre;
⁸And Assur joined with them, to help
 Lot's children they conspire.

⁹Do to them as to Midian,
 Jabin at Kison strand;
¹⁰And Sis'ra, which at En-dor fell,
 as dung to fat the land.

¹¹Like Oreb and like Zeeb make
 their noble men to fall;
Like Zeba and Zalmunna like,
 make thou their princes all;

¹²Who said, For our possession
 let us God's houses take.
¹³My God, them like a wheel, as chaff
 before the wind, them make.

¹⁴As fire consumes the wood, as flame
 doth mountains set on fire,
¹⁵Chase and affright them with the storm
 and tempest of thine ire.

¹⁶Their faces fill with shame, O Lord,
 that they may seek thy name.
¹⁷Let them confounded be, and vexed,
 and perish in their shame:

¹⁸That men may know that thou, to whom
 alone doth appertain
The name Jehovah, dost most high
 o'er all the earth remain.

Psalm 84

*To the chief Musician upon Gittith, A Psalm for the sons
of Korah.*

8,6,8,6

¹How lovely is thy dwelling-place,
    O Lord of hosts, to me!
The tabernacles of thy grace
    how pleasant, Lord, they be!

²My thirsty soul longs veh'mently,
    yea faints, thy courts to see:
My very heart and flesh cry out,
    O living God, for thee.

³Behold, the sparrow findeth out
    an house wherein to rest;
The swallow also for herself
    hath purchased a nest;

Ev'n thine own altars, where she safe
    her young ones forth may bring,
O thou almighty Lord of hosts,
    who art my God and King.

⁴Blessed are they in thy house that dwell,
    they ever give thee praise.
⁵Blessed is the man whose strength thou art,
    in whose heart are thy ways:

⁶Who passing thorough Baca's vale,
    therein do dig up wells;
Also the rain that falleth down
    the pools with water fills.

⁷So they from strength unwearied go
    still forward unto strength,
Until in Zion they appear
    before the Lord at length.

⁸Lord God of hosts, my prayer hear;
    O Jacob's God, give ear.
⁹See God our shield, look on the face
    of thine anointed dear.

[10]For in thy courts one day excels
   a thousand; rather in
My God's house will I keep a door,
   than dwell in tents of sin.

[11]For God the Lord's a sun and shield:
   he'll grace and glory give;
And will withhold no good from them
   that uprightly do live.

[12]O thou that art the Lord of hosts,
   that man is truly blessed,
Who by assured confidence
   on thee alone doth rest.

Psalm 85

To the chief Musician, A Psalm for the sons of Korah.

8,6,8,6

[1]O Lord, thou hast been favourable
   to thy beloved land:
Jacob's captivity thou hast
   recalled with mighty hand.

[2]Thou pardoned thy people hast
   all their iniquities;
Thou all their trespasses and sins
   hast covered from thine eyes.

[3]Thou took'st off all thine ire, and turn'dst
   from thy wrath's furiousness.
[4]Turn us, God of our health, and cause
   thy wrath 'gainst us to cease.

[5]Shall thy displeasure thus endure
   against us without end?
Wilt thou to generations all
   thine anger forth extend?

[6]That in thee may thy people joy,
   wilt thou not us revive?
[7]Show us thy mercy, Lord, to us
   do thy salvation give.

⁸I'll hear what God the Lord will speak:
    to his folk he'll speak peace,
And to his saints; but let them not
    return to foolishness.

⁹To them that fear him surely near
    is his salvation;
That glory in our land may have
    her habitation.

¹⁰Truth met with mercy, righteousness
    and peace kissed mutually:
¹¹Truth springs from earth, and righteousness
    looks down from heaven high.

¹²Yea, what is good the Lord shall give;
    our land shall yield increase:
¹³Justice, to set us in his steps,
    shall go before his face.

Psalm 86

A Prayer of David.

8,6,8,6

¹O Lord, do thou bow down thine ear,
    and hear me graciously;
Because I sore afflicted am,
    and am in poverty.

²Because I'm holy, let my soul
    by thee preserved be:
O thou my God, thy servant save,
    that puts his trust in thee.

³Sith unto thee I daily cry,
    be merciful to me.
⁴Rejoice thy servant's soul; for, Lord,
    I lift my soul to thee.

⁵For thou art gracious, O Lord,
    and ready to forgive;
And rich in mercy, all that call
    upon thee to relieve.

⁶Hear, Lord, my pray'r; unto the voice
　　of my request attend:
⁷In troublous times I'll call on thee;
　　for thou wilt answer send.

⁸Lord, there is none among the gods
　　that may with thee compare;
And like the works which thou hast done,
　　not any work is there.

⁹All nations whom thou mad'st shall come
　　and worship rev'rently
Before thy face; and they, O Lord,
　　thy name shall glorify.

¹⁰Because thou art exceeding great,
　　and works by thee are done
Which are to be admired; and thou
　　art God thyself alone.

¹¹Teach me thy way, and in thy truth,
　　O Lord, then walk will I;
Unite my heart, that I thy name
　　may fear continually.

¹²O Lord my God, with all my heart
　　to thee I will give praise;
And I the glory will ascribe
　　unto thy name always:

¹³Because thy mercy toward me
　　in greatness doth excel;
And thou delivered hast my soul
　　out from the lowest hell.

¹⁴O God, the proud against me rise,
　　and vi'lent men have met,
That for my soul have sought; and thee
　　before them have not set.

¹⁵But thou art full of pity, Lord,
　　a God most gracious,
Long-suffering, and in thy truth
　　and mercy plenteous.

¹⁶O turn to me thy countenance,
   and mercy on me have;
Thy servant strengthen, and the son
   of thine own handmaid save.

¹⁷Show me a sign for good, that they
   which do me hate may see,
And be ashamed; because thou, Lord,
   didst help and comfort me.

Psalm 87

A Psalm or Song for the sons of Korah.

                                       8,6,8,6

¹Upon the hills of holiness
   he his foundation sets.
²God, more than Jacob's dwellings all,
   delights in Zion's gates.

³Things glorious are said of thee,
   thou city of the Lord.
⁴Rahab and Babel I, to those
   that know me, will record:

Behold ev'n Tyrus, and with it
   the land of Palestine,
And likewise Ethiopia;
   this man was born therein.

⁵And it of Zion shall be said,
   This man and that man there
Was born; and he that is most High
   himself shall stablish her.

⁶When God the people writes, he'll count
   that this man born was there.
⁷There be that sing and play; and all
   my well-springs in thee are.

Psalm 88

A Song or Psalm for the sons of Korah, to the chief Musi-
cian upon Mahalath Leannoth, Maschil of Heman the
Ezrahite.

8,6,8,6

¹Lord God, my Saviour, day and night
before thee cried have I.
²Before thee let my prayer come;
give ear unto my cry.

³For troubles great do fill my soul;
my life draws nigh the grave.
⁴I'm counted with those that go down
to pit, and no strength have.

⁵Ev'n free among the dead, like them
that slain in grave do lie;
Cut off from thy hand, whom no more
thou hast in memory.

⁶Thou hast me laid in lowest pit,
in deeps and darksome caves.
⁷Thy wrath lies hard on me, thou hast
me pressed with all thy waves.

⁸Thou hast put far from me my friends,
thou mad'st them to abhor me;
And I am so shut up, that I
find no evasion for me.

⁹By reason of affliction
mine eye mourns dolefully:
To thee, Lord, do I call, and stretch
my hands continually.

¹⁰Wilt thou show wonders to the dead?
shall they rise, and thee bless?
¹¹Shall in the grave thy love be told?
in death thy faithfulness?

¹²Shall thy great wonders in the dark,
or shall thy righteousness
Be known to any in the land
of deep forgetfulness?

[13]But, Lord, to thee I cried; my pray'r
    at morn prevent shall thee.
[14]Why, Lord, dost thou cast off my soul,
    and hid'st thy face from me?

[15]Distressed am I, and from my youth
    I ready am to die;
Thy terrors I have borne, and am
    distracted fearfully.

[16]The dreadful fierceness of thy wrath
    quite over me doth go:
Thy terrors great have cut me off,
    they did pursue me so.

[17]For round about me ev'ry day,
    like water, they did roll;
And, gathering together, they
    have compassed my soul.

[18]My friends thou hast put far from me,
    and him that did me love;
And those that mine acquaintance were
    to darkness didst remove.

Psalm 89

Maschil of Ethan the Ezrahite.

8,6,8,6

[1]God's mercies I will ever sing;
    and with my mouth I shall
Thy faithfulness make to be known
    to generations all.

[2]For mercy shall be built, said I,
    for ever to endure;
Thy faithfulness, ev'n in the heav'ns,
    thou wilt establish sure.

[3]I with my chosen One have made
    a cov'nant graciously;
And to my servant, whom I loved,
    to David sworn have I;

⁴That I thy seed establish shall
   for ever to remain,
And will to generations all
   thy throne build and maintain.

⁵The praises of thy wonders, Lord,
   the heavens shall express;
And in the congregation
   of saints thy faithfulness.

⁶For who in heaven with the Lord
   may once himself compare?
Who is like God among the sons
   of those that mighty are?

⁷Great fear in meeting of the saints
   is due unto the Lord;
And he of all about him should
   with rev'rence be adored.

⁸O thou that art the Lord of hosts,
   what Lord in mightiness
Is like to thee? who compassed round
   art with thy faithfulness.

⁹Ev'n in the raging of the sea
   thou over it dost reign;
And when the waves thereof do swell,
   thou stillest them again.

¹⁰Rahab in pieces thou didst break,
   like one that slaughtered is;
And with thy mighty arm thou hast
   dispersed thine enemies.

¹¹The heav'ns are thine, thou for thine own
   the earth dost also take;
The world, and fullness of the same,
   thy pow'r did found and make.

¹²The north and south from thee alone
   their first beginning had;
Both Tabor mount and Hermon hill
   shall in thy name be glad.

[13]Thou hast an arm that's full of pow'r,
    thy hand is great in might;
And thy right hand exceedingly
    exalted is in height.

[14]Justice and judgment of thy throne
    are made the dwelling-place;
Mercy, accompanied with truth,
    shall go before thy face.

[15]O greatly blessed the people are
    the joyful sound that know;
In brightness of thy face, O Lord,
    they ever on shall go.

[16]They in thy name shall all the day
    rejoice exceedingly;
And in thy righteousness shall they
    exalted be on high.

[17]Because the glory of their strength
    doth only stand in thee;
And in thy favour shall our horn
    and pow'r exalted be.

[18]For God is our defence; and he
    to us doth safety bring:
The Holy One of Israel
    is our almighty King.

[19]In vision to thy Holy One
    thou saidst, I help upon
A strong one laid; out of the folk
    I raised a chosen one;

[20]Ev'n David, I have found him out
    a servant unto me;
And with my holy oil my King
    anointed him to be.

[21]With whom my hand shall stablished be;
    mine arm shall make him strong.
[22]On him the foe shall not exact,
    nor son of mischief wrong.

23I will beat down before his face
　　all his malicious foes;
I will them greatly plague who do
　　with hatred him oppose.

24My mercy and my faithfulness
　　with him yet still shall be;
And in my name his horn and pow'r
　　men shall exalted see.

25His hand and pow'r shall reach afar;
　　I'll set it in the sea;
And his right hand established
　　shall in the rivers be.

26Thou art my Father, he shall cry,
　　thou art my God alone;
And he shall say, Thou art the Rock
　　of my salvation.

27I'll make him my first-born, more high
　　than kings of any land.
28My love I'll ever keep for him,
　　my cov'nant fast shall stand.

29His seed I by my pow'r will make
　　for ever to endure;
And, as the days of heav'n, his throne
　　shall stable be, and sure.

30But if his children shall forsake
　　my laws, and go astray,
And in my judgments shall not walk,
　　but wander from my way:

31If they my laws break, and do not
　　keep my commandements;
32I'll visit then their faults with rods,
　　their sins with chastisements.

33Yet I'll not take my love from him,
　　nor false my promise make.
34My cov'nant I'll not break, nor change
　　what with my mouth I spake.

³⁵Once by my holiness I sware,
　　to David I'll not lie;
³⁶His seed and throne shall, as the sun,
　　before me last for aye.

³⁷It, like the moon, shall ever be
　　established stedfastly;
And like to that which in the heav'n
　　doth witness faithfully.

³⁸But thou, displeased, hast cast off,
　　thou didst abhor and loathe;
With him that thine anointed is
　　thou hast been very wroth.

³⁹Thou hast thy servant's covenant
　　made void, and quite cast by;
Thou hast profaned his crown, while it
　　cast on the ground doth lie.

⁴⁰Thou all his hedges hast broke down,
　　his strong holds down hast torn.
⁴¹He to all passers-by a spoil,
　　to neighbours is a scorn.

⁴²Thou hast set up his foes' right hand;
　　mad'st all his en'mies glad:
⁴³Turned his sword's edge, and him to stand
　　in battle hast not made.

⁴⁴His glory thou hast made to cease,
　　his throne to ground down cast;
⁴⁵Shortened his days of youth, and him
　　with shame thou covered hast.

⁴⁶How long, Lord, wilt thou hide thyself?
　　for ever, in thine ire?
And shall thine indignation
　　burn like unto a fire?

⁴⁷Remember, Lord, how short a time
　　I shall on earth remain:
O wherefore is it so that thou
　　has made all men in vain?

⁴⁸What man is he that liveth here,
and death shall never see?
Or from the power of the grave
what man his soul shall free?

⁴⁹Thy former loving-kindnesses,
O Lord, where be they now?
Those which in truth and faithfulness
to David sworn hast thou?

⁵⁰Mind, Lord, thy servant's sad reproach;
how I in bosom bear
The scornings of the people all,
who strong and mighty are.

⁵¹Wherewith thy raging enemies
reproached, O Lord, think on;
Wherewith they have reproached the steps
of thine anointed one.

⁵²All blessing to the Lord our God
let be ascribed then:
For evermore so let it be.
Amen, yea, and amen.

Psalm 90

A Prayer of Moses the man of God.

8,6,8,6

¹Lord, thou hast been our dwelling-place
in generations all.
²Before thou ever hadst brought forth
the mountains great or small;

Ere ever thou hadst formed the earth,
and all the world abroad;
Ev'n thou from everlasting art
to everlasting God.

³Thou dost unto destruction
man that is mortal turn;
And unto them thou say'st, Again,
ye sons of men, return.

⁴Because a thousand years appear
   no more before thy sight
Than yesterday, when it is past,
   or than a watch by night.

⁵As with an overflowing flood
   thou carry'st them away:
They like a sleep are, like the grass
   that grows at morn are they.

⁶At morn it flourishes and grows,
   cut down at ev'n doth fade.
⁷For by thine anger we're consumed,
   thy wrath makes us afraid.

⁸Our sins thou and iniquities
   dost in thy presence place,
And sett'st our secret faults before
   the brightness of thy face.

⁹For in thine anger all our days
   do pass on to an end;
And as a tale that hath been told,
   so we our years do spend.

¹⁰Threescore and ten years do sum up
   our days and years, we see;
Or, if, by reason of more strength,
   in some fourscore they be:

Yet doth the strength of such old men
   but grief and labour prove;
For it is soon cut off, and we
   fly hence, and soon remove.

¹¹Who knows the power of thy wrath?
   according to thy fear
¹²So is thy wrath: Lord, teach thou us
   our end in mind to bear;

And so to count our days, that we
   our hearts may still apply
To learn thy wisdom and thy truth,
   that we may live thereby.

¹³Turn yet again to us, O Lord,
   how long thus shall it be?
Let it repent thee now for those
   that servants are to thee.

¹⁴O with thy tender mercies, Lord,
   us early satisfy;
So we rejoice shall all our days,
   and still be glad in thee.

¹⁵According as the days have been,
   wherein we grief have had,
And years wherein we ill have seen,
   so do thou make us glad.

¹⁶O let thy work and pow'r appear
   thy servants' face before;
And show unto their children dear
   thy glory evermore:

¹⁷And let the beauty of the Lord
   our God be us upon:
Our handy-works establish thou,
   establish them each one.

Psalm 91

8,6,8,6

¹He that doth in the secret place
   of the most High reside,
Under the shade of him that is
   th' Almighty shall abide.

²I of the Lord my God will say,
   He is my refuge still,
He is my fortress, and my God,
   and in him trust I will.

³Assuredly he shall thee save,
   and give deliverance
From subtle fowler's snare, and from
   the noisome pestilence.

⁴His feathers shall thee hide; thy trust
   under his wings shall be:

His faithfulness shall be a shield
   and buckler unto thee.

5Thou shalt not need to be afraid
   for terrors of the night;
Nor for the arrow that doth fly
   by day, while it is light;

6Nor for the pestilence, that walks
   in darkness secretly;
Nor for destruction, that doth waste
   at noon-day openly.

7A thousand at thy side shall fall,
   on thy right hand shall lie
Ten thousand dead; yet unto thee
   it shall not once come nigh.

8Only thou with thine eyes shalt look,
   and a beholder be;
And thou therein the just reward
   of wicked men shalt see.

9Because the Lord, who constantly
   my refuge is alone,
Ev'n the most High, is made by thee
   thy habitation;

10No plague shall near thy dwelling come;
   no ill shall thee befall:
11For thee to keep in all thy ways
   his angels charge he shall.

12They in their hands shall bear thee up,
   still waiting thee upon;
Lest thou at any time should'st dash
   thy foot against a stone.

13Upon the adder thou shalt tread,
   and on the lion strong;
Thy feet on dragons trample shall,
   and on the lions young.

14Because on me he set his love,
   I'll save and set him free;

Because my great name he hath known,
    I will him set on high.

15He'll call on me, I'll answer him;
    I will be with him still
In trouble, to deliver him,
    and honour him I will.

16With length of days unto his mind
    I will him satisfy;
I also my salvation
    will cause his eyes to see.

Psalm 92

A Psalm or Song for the sabbath day.

8,6,8,6

1To render thanks unto the Lord
    it is a comely thing,
And to thy name, O thou most High,
    due praise aloud to sing.

2Thy loving-kindness to show forth
    when shines the morning light;
And to declare thy faithfulness
    with pleasure ev'ry night.

3On a ten-stringed instrument,
    upon the psaltery,
And on the harp with solemn sound,
    and grave sweet melody.

4For thou, Lord, by thy mighty works
    hast made my heart right glad;
And I will triumph in the works
    which by thine hands were made.

5How great, Lord, are thy works! each thought
    of thine a deep it is:
6A brutish man it knoweth not;
    fools understand not this.

7When those that lewd and wicked are
    spring quickly up like grass,

And workers of iniquity
   do flourish all apace;

It is that they for ever may
   destroyed be and slain;
8But thou, O Lord, art the most High,
   for ever to remain.

9For, lo, thine enemies, O Lord,
   thine en'mies perish shall;
The workers of iniquity
   shall be dispersed all.

10But thou shalt, like unto the horn
   of th' unicorn, exalt
My horn on high: thou with fresh oil
   anoint me also shalt.

11Mine eyes shall also my desire
   see on mine enemies;
Mine ears shall of the wicked hear
   that do against me rise.

12But like the palm-tree flourishing
   shall be the righteous one;
He shall like to the cedar grow
   that is in Lebanon.

13Those that within the house of God
   are planted by his grace,
They shall grow up, and flourish all
   in our God's holy place.

14And in old age, when others fade,
   they fruit still forth shall bring;
They shall be fat, and full of sap,
   and aye be flourishing;

15To show that upright is the Lord:
   he is a rock to me;
And he from all unrighteousness
   is altogether free.

Psalm 93

8,6,8,6

¹The Lord doth reign, and clothed is he
  with majesty most bright;
His works do show him clothed to be,
  and girt about with might.

The world is also stablished,
  that it cannot depart.
²Thy throne is fixed of old, and thou
  from everlasting art.

³The floods, O Lord, have lifted up,
  they lifted up their voice;
The floods have lifted up their waves,
  and made a mighty noise.

⁴But yet the Lord, that is on high,
  is more of might by far
Than noise of many waters is,
  or great sea-billows are.

⁵Thy testimonies ev'ry one
  in faithfulness excel;
And holiness for ever, Lord,
  thine house becometh well.

Psalm 94

8,6,8,6

¹O Lord God, unto whom alone
  all vengeance doth belong;
O mighty God, who vengeance own'st,
  shine forth, avenging wrong.

²Lift up thyself, thou of the earth
  the sov'reign Judge that art;
And unto those that are so proud
  a due reward impart.

³How long, O mighty God, shall they
  who lewd and wicked be,
How long shall they who wicked are
  thus triumph haughtily?

⁴How long shall things most hard by them
    be uttered and told?
And all that work iniquity
    to boast themselves be bold?

⁵Thy folk they break in pieces, Lord,
    thine heritage oppress:
⁶The widow they and stranger slay,
    and kill the fatherless.

⁷Yet say they, God it shall not see,
    nor God of Jacob know.
⁸Ye brutish people! understand;
    fools! when wise will ye grow?

⁹The Lord did plant the ear of man,
    and hear then shall not he?
He only formed the eye, and then
    shall he not clearly see?

¹⁰He that the nations doth correct,
    shall he not chastise you?
He knowledge unto man doth teach,
    and shall himself not know?

¹¹Man's thoughts to be but vanity
    the Lord doth well discern.
¹²Blessed is the man thou chast'nest, Lord,
    and mak'st thy law to learn:

¹³That thou may'st give him rest from days
    of sad adversity,
Until the pit be digged for those
    that work iniquity.

¹⁴For sure the Lord will not cast off
    those that his people be,
Neither his own inheritance
    quit and forsake will he:

¹⁵But judgment unto righteousness
    shall yet return again;
And all shall follow after it
    that are right-hearted men.

[16]Who will rise up for me against
    those that do wickedly?
Who will stand up for me 'gainst those
    that work iniquity?

[17]Unless the Lord had been my help
    when I was sore oppressed,
Almost my soul had in the house
    of silence been at rest.

[18]When I had uttered this word,
    (my foot doth slip away,)
Thy mercy held me up, O Lord,
    thy goodness did me stay.

[19]Amidst the multitude of thoughts
    which in my heart do fight,
My soul, lest it be overcharged,
    thy comforts do delight.

[20]Shall of iniquity the throne
    have fellowship with thee,
Which mischief, cunningly contrived,
    doth by a law decree?

[21]Against the righteous souls they join,
    they guiltless blood condemn.
[22]But of my refuge God's the rock,
    and my defence from them.

[23]On them their own iniquity
    the Lord shall bring and lay,
And cut them off in their own sin;
    our Lord God shall them slay.

Psalm 95

8,6,8,6

[1]O come, let us sing to the Lord:
    come, let us ev'ry one
A joyful noise make to the Rock
    of our salvation.

[2]Let us before his presence come
    with praise and thankful voice;

Let us sing psalms to him with grace,
   and make a joyful noise.

3For God, a great God, and great King,
   above all gods he is.
4Depths of the earth are in his hand,
   the strength of hills is his.

5To him the spacious sea belongs,
   for he the same did make;
The dry land also from his hands
   its form at first did take.

6O come, and let us worship him,
   let us bow down withal,
And on our knees before the Lord
   our Maker let us fall.

7For he's our God, the people we
   of his own pasture are,
And of his hand the sheep; to-day,
   if ye his voice will hear,

8Then harden not your hearts, as in
   the provocation,
As in the desert, on the day
   of the tentation:

9When me your fathers tempt'd and proved,
   and did my working see;
10Ev'n for the space of forty years
   this race hath grieved me.

I said, This people errs in heart,
   my ways they do not know:
11To whom I sware in wrath, that to
   my rest they should not go.

Psalm 96

8,6,8,6

1O sing a new song to the Lord:
   sing all the earth to God.
2To God sing, bless his name, show still
   his saving health abroad.

³Among the heathen nations
    his glory do declare;
And unto all the people show
    his works that wondrous are.

⁴For great's the Lord, and greatly he
    is to be magnified;
Yea, worthy to be feared is he
    above all gods beside.

⁵For all the gods are idols dumb,
    which blinded nations fear;
But our God is the Lord, by whom
    the heav'ns created were.

⁶Great honour is before his face,
    and majesty divine;
Strength is within his holy place,
    and there doth beauty shine.

⁷Do ye ascribe unto the Lord,
    of people ev'ry tribe,
Glory do ye unto the Lord,
    and mighty pow'r ascribe.

⁸Give ye the glory to the Lord
    that to his name is due;
Come ye into his courts, and bring
    an offering with you.

⁹In beauty of his holiness,
    O do the Lord adore;
Likewise let all the earth throughout
    tremble his face before.

¹⁰Among the heathen say, God reigns;
    the world shall steadfastly
Be fixed from moving; he shall judge
    the people righteously.

¹¹Let heav'ns be glad before the Lord,
    and let the earth rejoice;
Let seas, and all that is therein,
    cry out, and make a noise.

¹²Let fields rejoice, and ev'ry thing
    that springeth of the earth:
Then woods and ev'ry tree shall sing
    with gladness and with mirth

¹³Before the Lord; because he comes,
    to judge the earth comes he:
He'll judge the world with righteousness,
    the people faithfully.

Psalm 97

8,6,8,6

¹God reigneth, let the earth be glad,
    and isles rejoice each one.
²Dark clouds him compass; and in right
    with judgment dwells his throne.

³Fire goes before him, and his foes
    it burns up round about:
⁴His lightnings lighten did the world;
    earth saw, and shook throughout.

⁵Hills at the presence of the Lord,
    like wax, did melt away;
Ev'n at the presence of the Lord
    of all the earth, I say.

⁶The heav'ns declare his righteousness,
    all men his glory see.
⁷All who serve graven images,
    confounded let them be.

Who do of idols boast themselves,
    let shame upon them fall:
Ye that are called gods, see that
    ye do him worship all.

⁸Zion did hear, and joyful was,
    glad Judah's daughters were;
They much rejoiced, O Lord, because
    thy judgments did appear.

⁹For thou, O Lord, art high above
    all things on earth that are;

Above all other gods thou art
   exalted very far.

¹⁰Hate ill, all ye that love the Lord:
   his saints' souls keepeth he;
And from the hands of wicked men
   he sets them safe and free.

¹¹For all those that be righteous
   sown is a joyful light,
And gladness sown is for all those
   that are in heart upright.

¹²Ye righteous, in the Lord rejoice;
   express your thankfulness,
When ye into your memory
   do call his holiness.

Psalm 98

8,6,8,6

¹O sing a new song to the Lord,
   for wonders he hath done:
His right hand and his holy arm
   him victory hath won.

²The Lord God his salvation
   hath caused to be known;
His justice in the heathen's sight
   he openly hath shown.

³He mindful of his grace and truth
   to Isr'el's house hath been;
And the salvation of our God
   all ends of th' earth have seen.

⁴Let all the earth unto the Lord
   send forth a joyful noise;
Lift up your voice aloud to him,
   sing praises, and rejoice.

⁵With harp, with harp, and voice of psalms,
   unto Jehovah sing:
⁶With trumpets, cornets, gladly sound
   before the Lord the King.

⁷Let seas and all their fullness roar;
　　the world, and dwellers there;
⁸Let floods clap hands, and let the hills
　　together joy declare

⁹Before the Lord; because he comes,
　　to judge the earth comes he:
He'll judge the world with righteousness,
　　his folk with equity.

Psalm 99

8,6,8,6

¹Th' eternal Lord doth reign as king,
　　let all the people quake;
He sits between the cherubims,
　　let th' earth be moved and shake.

²The Lord in Zion great and high
　　above all people is;
³Thy great and dreadful name (for it
　　is holy) let them bless.

⁴The king's strength also judgment loves;
　　thou settlest equity:
Just judgment thou dost execute
　　in Jacob righteously.

⁵The Lord our God exalt on high,
　　and rev'rently do ye
Before his footstool worship him:
　　the Holy One is he.

⁶Moses and Aaron 'mong his priests,
　　Samuel, with them that call
Upon his name: these called on God,
　　and he them answer'd all.

⁷Within the pillar of the cloud
　　he unto them did speak:
The testimonies he them taught,
　　and laws, they did not break.

⁸Thou answer'dst them, O Lord our God;
　　thou wast a God that gave

Pardon to them, though on their deeds
    thou wouldest vengeance have.

[9]Do ye exalt the Lord our God,
    and at his holy hill
Do ye him worship: for the Lord
    our God is holy still.

Psalm 100

A Psalm of praise.

First Version (L.M.)
8,8,8,8

[1]All people that on earth do dwell,
Sing to the Lord with cheerful voice.
[2]Him serve with mirth, his praise forth tell,
    Come ye before him and rejoice.

[3]Know that the Lord is God indeed;
Without our aid he did us make:
We are his flock, he doth us feed,
    And for his sheep he doth us take.

[4]O enter then his gates with praise,
Approach with joy his courts unto:
Praise, laud, and bless his name always,
    For it is seemly so to do.

[5]For why? the Lord our God is good,
His mercy is for ever sure;
His truth at all times firmly stood,
And shall from age to age endure.

Psalm 100

Second Version (C.M.)
8,6,8,6

[1]O all ye lands, unto the Lord
    make ye a joyful noise.
[2]Serve God with gladness, him before
    come with a singing voice.

[3]Know ye the Lord that he is God;
    not we, but he us made:

We are his people, and the sheep
   within his pasture fed.

4Enter his gates and courts with praise,
   to thank him go ye thither:
To him express your thankfulness,
   and bless his name together.

5Because the Lord our God is good,
   his mercy faileth never;
And to all generations
   his truth endureth ever.

Psalm 101

A Psalm of David.

8,6,8,6

1I mercy will and judgment sing,
   Lord, I will sing to thee.
2With wisdom in a perfect way
   shall my behaviour be.

O when, in kindness unto me,
   wilt thou be pleas'd to come?
I with a perfect heart will walk
   within my house at home.

3I will endure no wicked thing
   before mine eyes to be:
I hate their work that turn aside,
   it shall not cleave to me.

4A stubborn and a froward heart
   depart quite from me shall;
A person giv'n to wickedness
   I will not know at all.

5I'll cut him off that slandereth
   his neighbour privily:
The haughty heart I will not bear,
   nor him that looketh high.

6Upon the faithful of the land
   mine eyes shall be, that they

May dwell with me: he shall me serve
    that walks in perfect way.

7Who of deceit a worker is
    in my house shall not dwell;
And in my presence shall he not
    remain that lies doth tell.

8Yea, all the wicked of the land
    early destroy will I;
All from God's city to cut off
    that work iniquity.

Psalm 102

*A Prayer of the afflicted, when he is overwhelmed, and
poureth out his
complaint before the Lord.*

First Version (C.M.)
8,6,8,6

1O Lord, unto my pray'r give ear,
    my cry let come to thee;
2And in the day of my distress
    hide not thy face from me.

Give ear to me; what time I call,
    to answer me make haste:
3For, as an hearth, my bones are burnt,
    my days, like smoke, do waste.

4My heart within me smitten is,
    and it is withered
Like very grass; so that I do
    forget to eat my bread.

5By reason of my groaning voice
    my bones cleave to my skin.
6Like pelican in wilderness
    forsaken I have been:

I like an owl in desert am,
    that nightly there doth moan;
7I watch, and like a sparrow am
    on the house-top alone.

[8]My bitter en'mies all the day
   reproaches cast on me;
And, being mad at me, with rage
   against me sworn they be.

[9]For why? I ashes eaten have
   like bread, in sorrows deep;
My drink I also mingled have
   with tears that I did weep.

[10]Thy wrath and indignation
   did cause this grief and pain;
For thou hast lift me up on high,
   and cast me down again.

[11]My days are like unto a shade,
   which doth declining pass;
And I am dried and withered,
   ev'n like unto the grass.

[12]But thou, Lord, everlasting art,
   and thy remembrance shall
Continually endure, and be
   to generations all.

[13]Thou shalt arise, and mercy have
   upon thy Zion yet;
The time to favour her is come,
   the time that thou hast set.

[14]For in her rubbish and her stones
   thy servants pleasure take;
Yea, they the very dust thereof
   do favour for her sake.

[15]So shall the heathen people fear
   the Lord's most holy name;
And all the kings on earth shall dread
   thy glory and thy fame.

[16]When Zion by the mighty Lord
   built up again shall be,
In glory then and majesty
   to men appear shall he.

[17]The prayer of the destitute
    he surely will regard;
Their prayer will he not despise,
    by him it shall be heard.

[18]For generations yet to come
    this shall be on record:
So shall the people that shall be
    created praise the Lord.

[19]He from his sanctuary's height
    hath downward cast his eye;
And from his glorious throne in heav'n
    the Lord the earth did spy;

[20]That of the mournful prisoner
    the groanings he might hear,
To set them free that unto death
    by men appointed are:

[21]That they in Zion may declare
    the Lord's most holy name,
And publish in Jerusalem
    the praises of the same;

[22]When as the people gather shall
    in troops with one accord,
When kingdoms shall assembled be
    to serve the highest Lord.

[23]My wonted strength and force he hath
    abated in the way,
And he my days hath shortened:
    [24]Thus therefore did I say,

My God, in mid-time of my days
    take thou me not away:
From age to age eternally
    thy years endure and stay.

[25]The firm foundation of the earth
    of old time thou hast laid;
The heavens also are the work
    which thine own hands have made.

26Thou shalt for evermore endure,
    but they shall perish all;
Yea, ev'ry one of them wax old,
    like to a garment, shall:

Thou, as a vesture, shalt them change,
    and they shall changed be:
27But thou the same art, and thy years
    are to eternity.

28The children of thy servants shall
    continually endure;
And in thy sight, O Lord, their seed
    shall be established sure.

Psalm 102

Second Version (L.M.)
8,8,8,8

1Lord, hear my pray'r, and let my cry
Have speedy access unto thee;
2In day of my calamity
    O hide not thou thy face from me.

Hear when I call to thee; that day
An answer speedily return:
3My days, like smoke, consume away,
    And, as an hearth, my bones do burn.

4My heart is wounded very sore,
And withered, like grass doth fade:
I am forgetful grown therefore
    To take and eat my daily bread.

5By reason of my smart within,
And voice of my most grievous groans,
My flesh consumed is, my skin,
    All parched, doth cleave unto my bones.

6The pelican of wilderness,
The owl in desert, I do match;
7And, sparrow-like, companionless,
    Upon the house's top, I watch.

[8]I all day long am made a scorn,
Reproached by my malicious foes:
The madmen are against me sworn,
    The men against me that arose.

[9]For I have ashes eaten up,
To me as if they had been bread;
And with my drink I in my cup
    Of bitter tears a mixture made.

[10]Because thy wrath was not appeased,
And dreadful indignation:
Therefore it was that thou me raised,
    And thou again didst cast me down.

[11]My days are like a shade alway,
Which doth declining swiftly pass;
And I am withered away,
    Much like unto the fading grass.

[12]But thou, O Lord, shalt still endure,
From change and all mutation free,
And to all generations sure
    Shall thy remembrance ever be.

[13]Thou shalt arise, and mercy yet
Thou to mount Zion shalt extend:
Her time for favour which was set,
    Behold, is now come to an end.

[14]Thy saints take pleasure in her stones,
Her very dust to them is dear.
[15]All heathen lands and kingly thrones
    On earth thy glorious name shall fear.

[16]God in his glory shall appear,
When Zion he builds and repairs.
[17]He shall regard and lend his ear
    Unto the needy's humble pray'rs:

Th' afflicted's pray'r he will not scorn.
[18]All times this shall be on record:
And generations yet unborn
    Shall praise and magnify the Lord.

¹⁹He from his holy place looked down,
The earth he viewed from heav'n on high;
²⁰To hear the pris'ner's mourning groan,
    And free them that are doomed to die;

²¹That Zion, and Jerus'lem too,
His name and praise may well record,
²²When people and the kingdoms do
    Assemble all to praise the Lord.

²³My strength he weakened in the way,
My days of life he shortened.
²⁴My God, O take me not away
    In mid-time of my days, I said:

Thy years throughout all ages last.
²⁵Of old thou hast established
The earth's foundation firm and fast:
    Thy mighty hands the heav'ns have made.

²⁶They perish shall, as garments do,
But thou shalt evermore endure;
As vestures, thou shalt change them so;
    And they shall all be changed sure:

²⁷But from all changes thou art free;
Thy endless years do last for aye.
²⁸Thy servants, and their seed who be,
Established shall before thee stay.

Psalm 103

A Psalm of David.

8,6,8,6

¹O thou my soul, bless God the Lord;
    and all that in me is
Be stirred up his holy name
    to magnify and bless.

²Bless, O my soul, the Lord thy God,
    and not forgetful be
Of all his gracious benefits
    he hath bestowed on thee.

³All thine iniquities who doth
  most graciously forgive:
Who thy diseases all and pains
  doth heal, and thee relieve.

⁴Who doth redeem thy life, that thou
  to death may'st not go down;
Who thee with loving-kindness doth
  and tender mercies crown:

⁵Who with abundance of good things
  doth satisfy thy mouth;
So that, ev'n as the eagle's age,
  renewed is thy youth.

⁶God righteous judgment executes
  for all oppressed ones.
⁷His ways to Moses, he his acts
  made known to Isr'el's sons.

⁸The Lord our God is merciful,
  and he is gracious,
Long-suffering, and slow to wrath,
  in mercy plenteous.

⁹He will not chide continually,
  nor keep his anger still.
¹⁰With us he dealt not as we sinned,
  nor did requite our ill.

¹¹For as the heaven in its height
  the earth surmounteth far;
So great to those that do him fear
  his tender mercies are:

¹²As far as east is distant from
  the west, so far hath he
From us removed, in his love,
  all our iniquity.

¹³Such pity as a father hath
  unto his children dear;
Like pity shows the Lord to such
  as worship him in fear.

¹⁴For he remembers we are dust,
    and he our frame well knows.
¹⁵Frail man, his days are like the grass,
    as flow'r in field he grows:

¹⁶For over it the wind doth pass,
    and it away is gone;
And of the place where once it was
    it shall no more be known.

¹⁷But unto them that do him fear
    God's mercy never ends;
And to their children's children still
    his righteousness extends:

¹⁸To such as keep his covenant,
    and mindful are alway
Of his most just commandements,
    that they may them obey.

¹⁹The Lord prepared hath his throne
    in heavens firm to stand;
And ev'ry thing that being hath
    his kingdom doth command.

²⁰O ye his angels, that excel
    in strength, bless ye the Lord;
Ye who obey what he commands,
    and hearken to his word.

²¹O bless and magnify the Lord,
    ye glorious hosts of his;
Ye ministers, that do fulfill
    whate'er his pleasure is.

²²O bless the Lord, all ye his works,
    wherewith the world is stored
In his dominions ev'ry where.
    My soul, bless thou the Lord.

Psalm 104

8,6,8,6

[1]Bless God, my soul. O Lord my God,
 thou art exceeding great;
With honour and with majesty
 thou clothed art in state.

[2]With light, as with a robe, thyself
 thou coverest about;
And, like unto a curtain, thou
 the heavens stretchest out.

[3]Who of his chambers doth the beams
 within the waters lay;
Who doth the clouds his chariot make,
 on wings of wind make way.

[4]Who flaming fire his ministers,
 his angels sp'rits, doth make:
[5]Who earth's foundations did lay,
 that it should never shake.

[6]Thou didst it cover with the deep,
 as with a garment spread:
The waters stood above the hills,
 when thou the word but said.

[7]But at the voice of thy rebuke
 they fled, and would not stay;
They at thy thunder's dreadful voice
 did haste them fast away.

[8]They by the mountains do ascend,
 and by the valley-ground
Descend, unto that very place
 which thou for them didst found.

[9]Thou hast a bound unto them set,
 that they may not pass over,
That they do not return again
 the face of earth to cover.

[10]He to the valleys sends the springs,
 which run among the hills:

[11]They to all beasts of field give drink,
   wild asses drink their fills.

[12]By them the fowls of heav'n shall have
   their habitation,
Which do among the branches sing
   with delectation.

[13]He from his chambers watereth
   the hills, when they are dried:
With fruit and increase of thy works
   the earth is satisfied.

[14]For cattle he makes grass to grow,
   he makes the herb to spring
For th' use of man, that food to him
   he from the earth may bring;

[15]And wine, that to the heart of man
   doth cheerfulness impart,
Oil that his face makes shine, and bread
   that strengtheneth his heart.

[16]The trees of God are full of sap;
   the cedars that do stand
In Lebanon, which planted were
   by his almighty hand.

[17]Birds of the air upon their boughs
   do choose their nests to make;
As for the stork, the fir-tree she
   doth for her dwelling take.

[18]The lofty mountains for wild goats
   a place of refuge be;
The conies also to the rocks
   do for their safety flee.

[19]He sets the moon in heav'n, thereby
   the seasons to discern:
From him the sun his certain time
   of going down doth learn.

[20]Thou darkness mak'st, 'tis night, then beasts
   of forests creep abroad.

²¹The lions young roar for their prey,
    and seek their meat from God.

²²The sun doth rise, and home they flock,
    down in their dens they lie.
²³Man goes to work, his labour he
    doth to the ev'ning ply.

²⁴How manifold, Lord, are thy works!
    in wisdom wonderful
Thou ev'ry one of them hast made;
    earth's of thy riches full:

²⁵So is this great and spacious sea,
    wherein things creeping are,
Which numbered cannot be; and beasts
    both great and small are there.

²⁶There ships go; there thou mak'st to play
    that leviathan great.
²⁷These all wait on thee, that thou may'st
    in due time give them meat.

²⁸That which thou givest unto them
    they gather for their food;
Thine hand thou open'st lib'rally,
    they filled are with good.

²⁹Thou hid'st thy face; they troubled are,
    their breath thou tak'st away;
Then do they die, and to their dust
    return again do they.

³⁰Thy quick'ning spirit thou send'st forth,
    then they created be;
And then the earth's decayed face
    renewed is by thee.

³¹The glory of the mighty Lord
    continue shall for ever:
The Lord Jehovah shall rejoice
    in all his works together.

³²Earth, as affrighted, trembleth all,
    if he on it but look;

And if the mountains he but touch,
    they presently do smoke.

[33]I will sing to the Lord most high,
    so long as I shall live;
And while I being have I shall
    to my God praises give.

[34]Of him my meditation shall
    sweet thoughts to me afford;
And as for me, I will rejoice
    in God, my only Lord.

[35]From earth let sinners be consumed,
    let ill men no more be.
O thou my soul, bless thou the Lord.
    Praise to the Lord give ye.

Psalm 105

8,6,8,6

[1]Give thanks to God, call on his name;
    to men his deeds make known.
[2]Sing ye to him, sing psalms; proclaim
    his wondrous works each one.

[3]See that ye in his holy name
    to glory do accord;
And let the heart of ev'ry one
    rejoice that seeks the Lord.

[4]The Lord Almighty, and his strength,
    with steadfast hearts seek ye:
His blessed and his gracious face
    seek ye continually.

[5]Think on the works that he hath done,
    which admiration breed;
His wonders, and the judgments all
    which from his mouth proceed;

[6]O ye that are of Abr'ham's race,
    his servant well approv'n;
And ye that Jacob's children are,
    whom he chose for his own.

⁷Because he, and he only, is
    the mighty Lord our God;
And his most righteous judgments are
    in all the earth abroad.

⁸His cov'nant he remembered hath,
    that it may ever stand:
To thousand generations
    the word he did command.

⁹Which covenant he firmly made
    with faithful Abraham,
And unto Isaac, by his oath,
    he did renew the same:

¹⁰And unto Jacob, for a law,
    he made it firm and sure,
A covenant to Israel,
    which ever should endure.

¹¹He said, I'll give Canaan's land
    for heritage to you;
¹²While they were strangers there, and few,
    in number very few:

¹³While yet they went from land to land
    without a sure abode;
And while through sundry kingdoms they
    did wander far abroad;

¹⁴Yet, notwithstanding suffer'd he
    no man to do them wrong:
Yea, for their sakes, he did reprove
    kings, who were great and strong.

¹⁵Thus did he say, Touch ye not those
    that mine anointed be,
Nor do the prophets any harm
    that do pertain to me.

¹⁶He called for famine on the land,
    he brake the staff of bread:
¹⁷But yet he sent a man before,
    by whom they should be fed;

Ev'n Joseph, whom unnat'rally
 sell for a slave did they;
[18]Whose feet with fetters they did hurt,
 and he in irons lay;

[19]Until the time that his word came
 to give him liberty;
The word and purpose of the Lord
 did him in prison try.

[20]Then sent the king, and did command
 that he enlarged should be:
He that the people's ruler was
 did send to set him free.

[21]A lord to rule his family
 he raised him, as most fit;
To him of all that he possessed
 he did the charge commit:

[22]That he might at his pleasure bind
 the princes of the land;
And he might teach his senators
 wisdom to understand.

[23]The people then of Israel
 down into Egypt came;
And Jacob also sojourned
 within the land of Ham.

[24]And he did greatly by his pow'r
 increase his people there;
And stronger than their enemies
 they by his blessing were.

[25]Their heart he turned to envy
 his folk maliciously,
With those that his own servants were
 to deal in subtlety.

[26]His servant Moses he did send,
 Aaron his chosen one.
[27]By these his signs and wonders great
 in Ham's land were made known.

²⁸Darkness he sent, and made it dark;
   his word they did obey.
²⁹He turned their waters into blood,
   and he their fish did slay.

³⁰The land in plenty brought forth frogs
   in chambers of their kings.
³¹His word all sorts of flies and lice
   in all their borders brings.

³²He hail for rain, and flaming fire
   into their land he sent:
³³And he their vines and fig-trees smote:
   trees of their coasts he rent.

³⁴He spake, and caterpillars came,
   locusts did much abound;
³⁵Which in their land all herbs consumed,
   and all fruits of their ground.

³⁶He smote all first-born in their land,
   chief of their strength each one.
³⁷With gold and silver brought them forth,
   weak in their tribes were none.

³⁸Egypt was glad when forth they went,
   their fear on them did light.
³⁹He spread a cloud for covering,
   and fire to shine by night.

⁴⁰They asked, and he brought quails: with bread
   of heav'n he filled them.
⁴¹He opened rocks, floods gushed, and ran
   in deserts like a stream.

⁴²For on his holy promise he,
   and servant Abr'ham, thought.
⁴³With joy his people, his elect
   with gladness, forth he brought.

⁴⁴And unto them the pleasant lands
   he of the heathen gave;
That of the people's labour they
   inheritance might have.

⁴⁵That they his statutes might observe
 according to his word;
And that they might his laws obey.
 Give praise unto the Lord.

Psalm 106

8,6,8,6

¹Give praise and thanks unto the Lord,
 for bountiful is he;
His tender mercy doth endure
 unto eternity.

²God's mighty works who can express?
 or show forth all his praise?
³Blessed are they that judgment keep,
 and justly do always.

⁴Remember me, Lord, with that love
 which thou to thine dost bear;
With thy salvation, O my God,
 to visit me draw near:

⁵That I thy chosen's good may see,
 and in their joy rejoice;
And may with thine inheritance
 triumph with cheerful voice.

⁶We with our fathers sinned have,
 and of iniquity
Too long we have the workers been;
 we have done wickedly.

⁷The wonders great, which thou, O Lord,
 didst work in Egypt land,
Our fathers, though they saw, yet them
 they did not understand:

And they thy mercies' multitude
 kept not in memory;
But at the sea, ev'n the Red sea,
 provoked him grievously.

⁸Nevertheless he saved them,
 ev'n for his own name's sake;

That so he might to be well known
    his mighty power make.

9When he the Red sea did rebuke,
    then dried up it was:
Through depths, as through the wilderness,
    he safely made them pass.

10From hands of those that hated them
    he did his people save;
And from the en'my's cruel hand
    to them redemption gave.

11The waters overwhelmed their foes;
    not one was left alive.
12Then they believed his word, and praise
    to him in songs did give.

13But soon did they his mighty works
    forget unthankfully,
And on his counsel and his will
    did not wait patiently;

14But much did lust in wilderness,
    and God in desert tempt.
15He gave them what they sought, but to
    their soul he leanness sent.

16And against Moses in the camp
    their envy did appear;
At Aaron they, the saint of God,
    envious also were.

17Therefore the earth did open wide,
    and Dathan did devour,
And all Abiram's company
    did cover in that hour.

18Likewise among their company
    a fire was kindled then;
And so the hot consuming flame
    burned up these wicked men.

19Upon the hill of Horeb they
    an idol-calf did frame,

A molten image they did make,
  and worshipped the same.

20And thus their glory, and their God,
  most vainly changed they
Into the likeness of an ox
  that eateth grass or hay.

21They did forget the mighty God,
  that had their saviour been,
By whom such great things brought to pass
  they had in Egypt seen.

22In Ham's land he did wondrous works,
  things terrible did he,
When he his mighty hand and arm
  stretched out at the Red sea.

23Then said he, He would them destroy,
  had not, his wrath to stay,
His chosen Moses stood in breach,
  that them he should not slay.

24Yea, they despised the pleasant land,
  believed not his word:
25But in their tents they murmured,
  not heark'ning to the Lord.

26Therefore in desert them to slay
  he lifted up his hand:
27'Mong nations to o'erthrow their seed,
  and scatter in each land.

28They unto Baal-peor did
  themselves associate;
The sacrifices of the dead
  they did profanely eat.

29Thus, by their lewd inventions,
  they did provoke his ire;
And then upon them suddenly
  the plague brake in as fire.

30Then Phin'has rose, and justice did,
  and so the plague did cease;

[31]That to all ages counted was
    to him for righteousness.

[32]And at the waters, where they strove,
    they did him angry make,
In such sort, that it fared ill
    with Moses for their sake:

[33]Because they there his spirit meek
    provoked bitterly,
So that he uttered with his lips
    words unadvisedly.

[34]Nor, as the Lord commanded them,
    did they the nations slay:
[35]But with the heathen mingled were,
    and learned of them their way.

[36]And they their idols served, which did
    a snare unto them turn.
[37]Their sons and daughters they to dev'ls
    in sacrifice did burn.

[38]In their own children's guiltless blood
    their hands they did imbrue,
Whom to Canaan's idols they
    for sacrifices slew:

So was the land defiled with blood.
    [39]They stained with their own way,
And with their own inventions
    a whoring they did stray.

[40]Against his people kindled was
    the wrath of God therefore,
Insomuch that he did his own
    inheritance abhor.

[41]He gave them to the heathen's hand;
    their foes did them command.
[42]Their en'mies them oppressed, they were
    made subject to their hand.

[43]He many times delivered them;
    but with their counsel so

They him provoked, that for their sin
 they were brought very low.

44Yet their affliction he beheld,
 when he did hear their cry:
45And he for them his covenant
 did call to memory;

After his mercies' multitude
 46he did repent: And made
Them to be pitied of all those
 who did them captive lead.

47O Lord our God, us save, and gather
 the heathen from among,
That we thy holy name may praise
 in a triumphant song.

48Blessed be Jehovah, Isr'el's God,
 to all eternity:
Let all the people say, Amen.
 Praise to the Lord give ye.

Psalm 107

8,6,8,6

1Praise God, for he is good: for still
 his mercies lasting be.
2Let God's redeemed say so, whom he
 from th' en'my's hand did free;

3And gathered them out of the lands,
 from north, south, east, and west.
4They strayed in desert's pathless way,
 no city found to rest.

5For thirst and hunger in them faints
 6their soul. When straits them press,
They cry unto the Lord, and he
 them frees from their distress.

7Them also in a way to walk
 that right is he did guide,
That they might to a city go,
 wherein they might abide.

[8]O that men to the Lord would give
    praise for his goodness then,
And for his works of wonder done
    unto the sons of men!

[9]For he the soul that longing is
    doth fully satisfy;
With goodness he the hungry soul
    doth fill abundantly.

[10]Such as shut up in darkness deep,
    and in death's shade abide,
Whom strongly hath affliction bound,
    and irons fast have tied:

[11]Because against the words of God
    they wrought rebelliously,
And they the counsel did contemn
    of him that is most High:

[12]Their heart he did bring down with grief,
    they fell, no help could have.
[13]In trouble then they cried to God,
    he them from straits did save.

[14]He out of darkness did them bring,
    and from death's shade them take;
These bands, wherewith they had been bound,
    asunder quite he brake.

[15]O that men to the Lord would give
    praise for his goodness then,
And for his works of wonder done
    unto the sons of men!

[16]Because the mighty gates of brass
    in pieces he did tear,
By him in sunder also cut
    the bars of iron were.

[17]Fools, for their sin, and their offence,
    do sore affliction bear;
[18]All kind of meat their soul abhors;
    they to death's gates draw near.

¹⁹In grief they cry to God; he saves
    them from their miseries.
²⁰He sends his word, them heals, and them
    from their destructions frees.

²¹O that men to the Lord would give
    praise for his goodness then,
And for his works of wonder done
    unto the sons of men!

²²And let them sacrifice to him
    off'rings of thankfulness;
And let them show abroad his works
    in songs of joyfulness.

²³Who go to sea in ships, and in
    great waters trading be,
²⁴Within the deep these men God's works
    and his great wonders see.

²⁵For he commands, and forth in haste
    the stormy tempest flies,
Which makes the sea with rolling waves
    aloft to swell and rise.

²⁶They mount to heav'n, then to the depths
    they do go down again;
Their soul doth faint and melt away
    with trouble and with pain.

²⁷They reel and stagger like one drunk,
    at their wit's end they be:
²⁸Then they to God in trouble cry,
    who them from straits doth free.

²⁹The storm is changed into a calm
    at his command and will;
So that the waves, which raged before,
    now quiet are and still.

³⁰Then are they glad, because at rest
    and quiet now they be:
So to the haven he them brings,
    which they desired to see.

³¹O that men to the Lord would give
    praise for his goodness then,
And for his works of wonder done
    unto the sons of men!

³²Among the people gathered
    let them exalt his name;
Among assembled elders spread
    his most renowned fame.

³³He to dry land turns water-springs,
    and floods to wilderness;
³⁴For sins of those that dwell therein,
    fat land to barrenness.

³⁵The burnt and parched wilderness
    to water-pools he brings;
The ground that was dried up before
    he turns to water-springs:

³⁶And there, for dwelling, he a place
    doth to the hungry give,
That they a city may prepare
    commodiously to live.

³⁷There sow they fields, and vineyards plant,
    to yield fruits of increase.
³⁸His blessing makes them multiply,
    lets not their beasts decrease.

³⁹Again they are diminished,
    and very low brought down,
Through sorrow and affliction,
    and great oppression.

⁴⁰He upon princes pours contempt,
    and causeth them to stray,
And wander in a wilderness,
    wherein there is no way.

⁴¹Yet setteth he the poor on high
    from all his miseries,
And he, much like unto a flock,
    doth make him families.

⁴²They that are righteous shall rejoice,
   when they the same shall see;
And, as ashamed, stop her mouth
   shall all iniquity.

⁴³Whoso is wise, and will these things
   observe, and them record,
Ev'n they shall understand the love
   and kindness of the Lord.

Psalm 108

A Song or Psalm of David.

8,6,8,6

¹My heart is fixed, Lord; I will sing,
   and with my glory praise.
²Awake up psaltery and harp;
   myself I'll early raise.

³I'll praise thee 'mong the people, Lord;
   'mong nations sing will I:
⁴For above heav'n thy mercy's great,
   thy truth doth reach the sky.

⁵Be thou above the heavens, Lord,
   exalted gloriously;
Thy glory all the earth above
   be lifted up on high.

⁶That those who thy beloved are
   delivered may be,
O do thou save with thy right hand,
   and answer give to me.

⁷God in his holiness hath said,
   Herein I will take pleasure;
Shechem I will divide, and forth
   will Succoth's valley measure.

⁸Gilead I claim as mine by right;
   Manasseh mine shall be;
Ephraim is of my head the strength;
   Judah gives laws for me;

⁹Moab's my washing-pot; my shoe
   I'll over Edom throw;
Over the land of Palestine
   I will in triumph go.

¹⁰O who is he will bring me to
   the city fortified?
O who is he that to the land
   of Edom will me guide?

¹¹O God, thou who hadst cast us off,
   this thing wilt thou not do?
And wilt not thou, ev'n thou, O God,
   forth with our armies go?

¹²Do thou from trouble give us help,
   for helpless is man's aid.
¹³Through God we shall do valiantly;
   our foes he shall down tread.

Psalm 109

To the chief Musician, A Psalm of David.

8,6,8,6

¹O thou the God of all my praise,
   do thou not hold thy peace;
²For mouths of wicked men to speak
   against me do not cease:

The mouths of vile deceitful men
   against me opened be;
And with a false and lying tongue
   they have accused me.

³They did beset me round about
   with words of hateful spight:
And though to them no cause I gave,
   against me they did fight.

⁴They for my love became my foes,
   but I me set to pray.
⁵Evil for good, hatred for love,
   to me they did repay.

⁶Set thou the wicked over him;
　　and upon his right hand
Give thou his greatest enemy,
　　ev'n Satan, leave to stand.

⁷And when by thee he shall be judged,
　　let him condemned be;
And let his pray'r be turned to sin,
　　when he shall call on thee.

⁸Few be his days, and in his room
　　his charge another take.
⁹His children let be fatherless,
　　his wife a widow make.

¹⁰His children let be vagabonds,
　　and beg continually;
And from their places desolate
　　seek bread for their supply.

¹¹Let covetous extortioners
　　catch all he hath away:
Of all for which he laboured hath
　　let strangers make a prey.

¹²Let there be none to pity him,
　　let there be none at all
That on his children fatherless
　　will let his mercy fall.

¹³Let his posterity from earth
　　cut off for ever be,
And in the foll'wing age their name
　　be blotted out by thee.

¹⁴Let God his father's wickedness
　　still to remembrance call;
And never let his mother's sin
　　be blotted out at all.

¹⁵But let them all before the Lord
　　appear continually,
That he may wholly from the earth
　　cut off their memory.

¹⁶Because he mercy minded not,
    but persecuted still
The poor and needy, that he might
    the broken-hearted kill.

¹⁷As he in cursing pleasure took,
    so let it to him fall;
As he delighted not to bless,
    so bless him not at all.

¹⁸As cursing he like clothes put on,
    into his bowels so,
Like water, and into his bones,
    like oil, down let it go.

¹⁹Like to the garment let it be
    which doth himself array,
And for a girdle, wherewith he
    is girt about alway.

²⁰From God let this be their reward
    that en'mies are to me,
And their reward that speak against
    my soul maliciously.

²¹But do thou, for thine own name's sake,
    O God the Lord, for me:
Sith good and sweet thy mercy is,
    from trouble set me free.

²²For I am poor and indigent,
    afflicted sore am I,
My heart within me also is
    wounded exceedingly.

²³I pass like a declining shade,
    am like the locust tost:
²⁴My knees through fasting weakened are,
    my flesh hath fatness lost.

²⁵I also am a vile reproach
    unto them made to be;
And they that did upon me look
    did shake their heads at me.

²⁶O do thou help and succour me,
    who art my God and Lord:
And, for thy tender mercy's sake,
    safety to me afford:

²⁷That thereby they may know that this
    is thy almighty hand;
And that thou, Lord, hast done the same,
    they may well understand.

²⁸Although they curse with spite, yet, Lord,
    bless thou with loving voice:
Let them ashamed be when they rise;
    thy servant let rejoice.

²⁹Let thou mine adversaries all
    with shame be clothed over;
And let their own confusion
    them, as a mantle, cover.

³⁰But as for me, I with my mouth
    will greatly praise the Lord;
And I among the multitude
    his praises will record.

³¹For he shall stand at his right hand
    who is in poverty,
To save him from all those that would
    condemn his soul to die.

Psalm 110

A Psalm of David.

8,6,8,6

¹The Lord did say unto my Lord,
    Sit thou at my right hand,
Until I make thy foes a stool,
    whereon thy feet may stand.

²The Lord shall out of Zion send
    the rod of thy great pow'r:
In midst of all thine enemies
    be thou the governor.

³A willing people in thy day
    of pow'r shall come to thee,
In holy beauties from morn's womb;
    thy youth like dew shall be.

⁴The Lord himself hath made an oath,
    and will repent him never,
Of th' order of Melchizedek
    thou art a priest for ever.

⁵The glorious and mighty Lord,
    that sits at thy right hand,
Shall, in his day of wrath, strike through
    kings that do him withstand.

⁶He shall among the heathen judge,
    he shall with bodies dead
The places fill: o'er many lands
    he wound shall ev'ry head.

⁷The brook that runneth in the way
    with drink shall him supply;
And, for this cause, in triumph he
    shall lift his head on high.

Psalm 111

8,6,8,6

¹Praise ye the Lord: with my whole heart
    I will God's praise declare,
Where the assemblies of the just
    and congregations are.

²The whole works of the Lord our God
    are great above all measure,
Sought out they are of ev'ry one
    that doth therein take pleasure.

³His work most honourable is,
    most glorious and pure,
And his untainted righteousness
    for ever doth endure.

⁴His works most wonderful he hath
    made to be thought upon:

The Lord is gracious, and he is
    full of compassion.

⁵He giveth meat unto all those
    that truly do him fear;
And evermore his covenant
    he in his mind will bear.

⁶He did the power of his works
    unto his people show,
When he the heathen's heritage
    upon them did bestow.

⁷His handy-works are truth and right;
    all his commands are sure:
⁸And, done in truth and uprightness,
    they evermore endure.

⁹He sent redemption to his folk;
    his covenant for aye
He did command: holy his name
    and rev'rend is alway.

¹⁰Wisdom's beginning is God's fear:
    good understanding they
Have all that his commands fulfill:
    his praise endures for aye.

Psalm 112

8,6,8,6

¹Praise ye the Lord. The man is blessed
    that fears the Lord aright,
He who in his commandements
    doth greatly take delight.

²His seed and offspring powerful
    shall be the earth upon:
Of upright men blessed shall be
    the generation.

³Riches and wealth shall ever be
    within his house in store;
And his unspotted righteousness
    endures for evermore.

⁴Unto the upright light doth rise,
    though he in darkness be:
Compassionate, and merciful,
    and righteous, is he.

⁵A good man doth his favour show,
    and doth to others lend:
He with discretion his affairs
    will guide unto the end.

⁶Surely there is not any thing
    that ever shall him move:
The righteous man's memorial
    shall everlasting prove.

⁷When he shall evil tidings hear,
    he shall not be afraid:
His heart is fixed, his confidence
    upon the Lord is stayed.

⁸His heart is firmly stablished,
    afraid he shall not be,
Until upon his enemies
    he his desire shall see.

⁹He hath dispersed, giv'n to the poor;
    his righteousness shall be
To ages all; with honour shall
    his horn be raised high.

¹⁰The wicked shall it see, and fret,
    his teeth gnash, melt away:
What wicked men do most desire
    shall utterly decay.

Psalm 113

8,6,8,6

¹Praise God: ye servants of the Lord,
    O praise, the Lord's name praise.
²Yea, blessed be the name of God
    from this time forth always.

³From rising sun to where it sets,
    God's name is to be praised.

[4]Above all nations God is high,
  'bove heav'ns his glory raised.

[5]Unto the Lord our God that dwells
  on high, who can compare?
[6]Himself that humbleth things to see
  in heav'n and earth that are.

[7]He from the dust doth raise the poor,
  that very low doth lie;
And from the dunghill lifts the man
  oppressed with poverty;

[8]That he may highly him advance,
  and with the princes set;
With those that of his people are
  the chief, ev'n princes great.

[9]The barren woman house to keep
  he maketh, and to be
Of sons a mother full of joy.
  Praise to the Lord give ye.

Psalm 114

8,6,8,6

[1]When Isr'el out of Egypt went,
  and did his dwelling change,
When Jacob's house went out from those
  that were of language strange,

[2]He Judah did his sanctuary,
  his kingdom Isr'el make:
[3]The sea it saw, and quickly fled,
  Jordan was driven back.

[4]Like rams the mountains, and like lambs
  the hills skipped to and fro.
[5]O sea, why fledd'st thou? Jordan, back
  why wast thou driven so?

[6]Ye mountains great, wherefore was it
  that ye did skip like rams?
And wherefore was it, little hills,
  that ye did leap like lambs?

⁷O at the presence of the Lord,
    earth, tremble thou for fear,
While as the presence of the God
    of Jacob doth appear:

⁸Who from the hard and stony rock
    did standing water bring;
And by his pow'r did turn the flint
    into a water-spring.

Psalm 115

8,6,8,6

¹Not unto us, Lord, not to us,
    but do thou glory take
Unto thy name, ev'n for thy truth,
    and for thy mercy's sake.

²O wherefore should the heathen say,
    Where is their God now gone?
³But our God in the heavens is,
    what pleased him he hath done.

⁴Their idols silver are and gold,
    work of men's hands they be.
⁵Mouths have they, but they do not speak;
    and eyes, but do not see;

⁶Ears have they, but they do not hear;
    noses, but savour not;
⁷Hands, feet, but handle not, nor walk;
    nor speak they through their throat.

⁸Like them their makers are, and all
    on them their trust that build.
⁹O Isr'el, trust thou in the Lord,
    he is their help and shield.

¹⁰O Aaron's house, trust in the Lord,
    their help and shield is he.
¹¹Ye that fear God, trust in the Lord,
    their help and shield he'll be.

¹²The Lord of us hath mindful been,
    and he will bless us still:

He will the house of Isr'el bless,
   bless Aaron's house he will.

13Both small and great, that fear the Lord,
   he will them surely bless.
14The Lord will you, you and your seed,
   aye more and more increase.

15O blessed are ye of the Lord,
   who made the earth and heav'n.
16The heav'n, ev'n heav'ns, are God's, but he
   earth to men's sons hath giv'n.

17The dead, nor who to silence go,
   God's praise do not record.
18But henceforth we for ever will
   bless God. Praise ye the Lord.

Psalm 116

8,6,8,6

1I love the Lord, because my voice
   and prayers he did hear.
2I, while I live, will call on him,
   who bowed to me his ear.

3Of death the cords and sorrows did
   about me compass round;
The pains of hell took hold on me,
   I grief and trouble found.

4Upon the name of God the Lord
   then did I call, and say,
Deliver thou my soul, O Lord,
   I do thee humbly pray.

5God merciful and righteous is,
   yea, gracious is our Lord.
6God saves the meek: I was brought low,
   he did me help afford.

7O thou my soul, do thou return
   unto thy quiet rest;
For largely, lo, the Lord to thee
   his bounty hath expressed.

⁸For my distressed soul from death
   delivered was by thee:
Thou didst my mourning eyes from tears,
   my feet from falling, free.

⁹I in the land of those that live
   will walk the Lord before.
¹⁰I did believe, therefore I spake:
   I was afflicted sore.

¹¹I said, when I was in my haste,
   that all men liars be.
¹²What shall I render to the Lord
   for all his gifts to me?

¹³I'll of salvation take the cup,
   on God's name will I call:
¹⁴I'll pay my vows now to the Lord
   before his people all.

¹⁵Dear in God's sight is his saints' death.
   ¹⁶Thy servant, Lord, am I;
Thy servant sure, thine handmaid's son:
   my bands thou didst untie.

¹⁷Thank-off'rings I to thee will give,
   and on God's name will call.
¹⁸I'll pay my vows now to the Lord
   before his people all;

¹⁹Within the courts of God's own house,
   within the midst of thee,
O city of Jerusalem.
   Praise to the Lord give ye.

Psalm 117

8,6,8,6

¹O give ye praise unto the Lord,
   all nations that be;
Likewise, ye people all, accord
   his name to magnify.

²For great to us-ward ever are
    his loving-kindnesses:
His truth endures for evermore.
    The Lord O do ye bless.

Psalm 118

8,6,8,6

¹O praise the Lord, for he is good;
    his mercy lasteth ever.
²Let those of Israel now say,
    His mercy faileth never.

³Now let the house of Aaron say,
    His mercy lasteth ever.
⁴Let those that fear the Lord now say,
    His mercy faileth never.

⁵I in distress called on the Lord;
    the Lord did answer me:
He in a large place did me set,
    from trouble made me free.

⁶The mighty Lord is on my side,
    I will not be afraid;
For any thing that man can do
    I shall not be dismayed.

⁷The Lord doth take my part with them
    that help to succour me:
Therefore on those that do me hate
    I my desire shall see.

⁸Better it is to trust in God
    than trust in man's defence;
⁹Better to trust in God than make
    princes our confidence.

¹⁰The nations, joining all in one,
    did compass me about:
But in the Lord's most holy name
    I shall them all root out.

¹¹They compassed me about; I say,
    they compassed me about:

But in the Lord's most holy name
   I shall them all root out.

12Like bees they compassed me about;
   like unto thorns that flame
They quenched are: for them shall I
   destroy in God's own name.

13Thou sore hast thrust, that I might fall,
   but my Lord helped me.
14God my salvation is become,
   my strength and song is he.

15In dwellings of the righteous
   is heard the melody
Of joy and health: the Lord's right hand
   doth ever valiantly.

16The right hand of the mighty Lord
   exalted is on high;
The right hand of the mighty Lord
   doth ever valiantly.

17I shall not die, but live, and shall
   the works of God discover.
18The Lord hath me chastised sore,
   but not to death giv'n over.

19O set ye open unto me
   the gates of righteousness;
Then will I enter into them,
   and I the Lord will bless.

20This is the gate of God, by it
   the just shall enter in.
21Thee will I praise, for thou me heard'st
   and hast my safety been.

22That stone is made head corner-stone,
   which builders did despise:
23This is the doing of the Lord,
   and wondrous in our eyes.

24This is the day God made, in it
   we'll joy triumphantly.

²⁵Save now, I pray thee, Lord; I pray,
    send now prosperity.

²⁶Blessed is he in God's great name
    that cometh us to save:
We, from the house which to the Lord
    pertains, you blessed have.

²⁷God is the Lord, who unto us
    hath made light to arise:
Bind ye unto the altar's horns
    with cords the sacrifice.

²⁸Thou art my God, I'll thee exalt;
    my God, I will thee praise.
²⁹Give thanks to God, for he is good:
    his mercy lasts always.

Psalm 119
Aleph, The 1st Part

8,6,8,6

¹Blessed are they that undefiled,
    and straight are in the way;
Who in the Lord's most holy law
    do walk, and do not stray.

²Blessed are they who to observe
    his statutes are inclined;
And who do seek the living God
    with their whole heart and mind.

³Such in his ways do walk, and they
    do no iniquity.
⁴Thou hast commanded us to keep
    thy precepts carefully.

⁵O that thy statutes to observe
    thou would'st my ways direct!
⁶Then shall I not be shamed, when I
    thy precepts all respect.

⁷Then with integrity of heart
    thee will I praise and bless,

When I the judgments all have learned
    of thy pure righteousness.

8That I will keep thy statutes all
    firmly resolved have I:
O do not then, most gracious God,
    forsake me utterly.

Psalm 119
Beth, The 2nd Part

8,6,8,6

9By what means shall a young man learn
    his way to purify?
If he according to thy word
    thereto attentive be.

10Unfeignedly thee have I sought
    with all my soul and heart:
O let me not from the right path
    of thy commands depart.

11Thy word I in my heart have hid,
    that I offend not thee.
12O Lord, thou ever blessed art,
    thy statutes teach thou me.

13The judgments of thy mouth each one
    my lips declared have:
14More joy thy testimonies' way
    than riches all me gave.

15I will thy holy precepts make
    my meditation;
And carefully I'll have respect
    unto thy ways each one.

16Upon thy statutes my delight
    shall constantly be set:
And, by thy grace, I never will
    thy holy word forget.

Psalm 119
Gimel, The 3rd Part

8,6,8,6

[17]With me thy servant, in thy grace,
   deal bountifully, Lord:
That by thy favor I may live,
   and duly keep thy word.

[18]Open mine eyes, that of thy law
   the wonders I may see.
[19]I am a stranger on this earth,
   hide not thy laws from me.

[20]My soul within me breaks, and doth
   much fainting still endure,
Through longing that it hath all times
   unto thy judgments pure.

[21]Thou hast rebuked the cursed proud,
   who from thy precepts swerve.
[22]Reproach and shame remove from me,
   for I thy laws observe.

[23]Against me princes spake with spite,
   while they in council sat:
But I thy servant did upon
   thy statutes meditate.

[24]My comfort, and my heart's delight,
   thy testimonies be;
And they, in all my doubts and fears,
   are counsellors to me.

Psalm 119
Daleth, The 4th Part

8,6,8,6

[25]My soul to dust cleaves: quicken me,
   according to thy word.
[26]My ways I showed, and me thou heard'st:
   teach me thy statutes, Lord.

[27]The way of thy commandements
   make me aright to know;

So all thy works that wondrous are
   I shall to others show.

28My soul doth melt, and drop away,
   for heaviness and grief:
To me, according to thy word,
   give strength, and send relief.

29From me the wicked way of lies
   let far removed be;
And graciously thy holy law
   do thou grant unto me.

30I chosen have the perfect way
   of truth and verity:
Thy judgments that most righteous are
   before me laid have I.

31I to thy testimonies cleave;
   shame do not on me cast.
32I'll run thy precepts' way, when thou
   my heart enlarged hast.

Psalm 119
He, The 5th Part

8,6,8,6

33Teach me, O Lord, the perfect way
   of thy precepts divine,
And to observe it to the end
   I shall my heart incline.

34Give understanding unto me,
   so keep thy law shall I;
Yea, ev'n with my whole heart I shall
   observe it carefully.

35In thy law's path make me to go;
   for I delight therein.
36My heart unto thy testimonies,
   and not to greed, incline.

37Turn thou away my sight and eyes
   from viewing vanity;

And in thy good and holy way
   be pleased to quicken me.

[38]Confirm to me thy gracious word,
   which I did gladly hear,
Ev'n to thy servant, Lord, who is
   devoted to thy fear.

[39]Turn thou away my feared reproach;
   for good thy judgments be.
[40]Lo, for thy precepts I have longed;
   in thy truth quicken me.

Psalm 119
Vau, The 6th Part

8,6,8,6

[41]Let thy sweet mercies also come
   and visit me, O Lord;
Ev'n thy benign salvation,
   according to thy word.

[42]So shall I have wherewith I may
   give him an answer just,
Who spitefully reproacheth me;
   for in thy word I trust.

[43]The word of truth out of my mouth
   take thou not utterly;
For on thy judgments righteous
   my hope doth still rely.

[44]So shall I keep for evermore
   thy law continually.
[45]And, sith that I thy precepts seek,
   I'll walk at liberty.

[46]I'll speak thy word to kings, and I
   with shame shall not be moved;
[47]And will delight myself always
   in thy laws, which I loved.

⁴⁸To thy commandments, which I loved,
    my hands lift up I will;
And I will also meditate
    upon thy statutes still.

Psalm 119
Zain, The 7th Part

8,6,8,6

⁴⁹Remember, Lord, thy gracious word
    thou to thy servant spake,
Which, for a ground of my sure hope,
    thou causedst me to take.

⁵⁰This word of thine my comfort is
    in mine affliction:
For in my straits I am revived
    by this thy word alone.

⁵¹The men whose hearts with pride are stuffed
    did greatly me deride;
Yet from thy straight commandements
    I have not turned aside.

⁵²Thy judgments righteous, O Lord,
    which thou of old forth gave,
I did remember, and myself
    by them comforted have.

⁵³Horror took hold on me, because
    ill men thy law forsake.
⁵⁴I in my house of pilgrimage
    thy laws my songs do make.

⁵⁵Thy name by night, Lord, I did mind,
    and I have kept thy law.
⁵⁶And this I had, because thy word
    I kept, and stood in awe.

Psalm 119
Cheth, The 8th Part

8,6,8,6

⁵⁷Thou my sure portion art alone,
　which I did choose, O Lord:
I have resolved, and said, that I
　would keep thy holy word.

⁵⁸With my whole heart I did entreat
　thy face and favour free:
According to thy gracious word
　be merciful to me.

⁵⁹I thought upon my former ways,
　and did my life well try;
And to thy testimonies pure
　my feet then turned I.

⁶⁰I did not stay, nor linger long,
　as those that slothful are;
But hastily thy laws to keep
　myself I did prepare.

⁶¹Bands of ill men me robbed; yet I
　thy precepts did not slight.
⁶²I'll rise at midnight thee to praise,
　ev'n for thy judgments right.

⁶³I am companion to all those
　who fear, and thee obey.
⁶⁴O Lord, thy mercy fills the earth:
　teach me thy laws, I pray.

Psalm 119
Teth, The 9th Part

8,6,8,6

⁶⁵Well hast thou with thy servant dealt,
　as thou didst promise give.
⁶⁶Good judgment me, and knowledge teach,
　for I thy word believe.

⁶⁷Ere I afflicted was I strayed;
　but now I keep thy word.

⁶⁸Both good thou art, and good thou do'st:
    teach me thy statutes, Lord.

⁶⁹The men that are puffed up with pride
    against me forged a lie;
Yet thy commandements observe
    with my whole heart will I.

⁷⁰Their hearts, through worldly ease and wealth,
    as fat as grease they be:
But in thy holy law I take
    delight continually.

⁷¹It hath been very good for me
    that I afflicted was,
That I might well instructed be,
    and learn thy holy laws.

⁷²The word that cometh from thy mouth
    is better unto me
Than many thousands and great sums
    of gold and silver be.

Psalm 119
Jod, The 10th Part

8,6,8,6

⁷³Thou mad'st and fashion'dst me: thy laws
    to know give wisdom, Lord.
⁷⁴So who thee fear shall joy to see
    me trusting in thy word.

⁷⁵That very right thy judgments are
    I know, and do confess;
And that thou hast afflicted me
    in truth and faithfulness.

⁷⁶O let thy kindness merciful,
    I pray thee, comfort me,
As to thy servant faithfully
    was promised by thee.

⁷⁷And let thy tender mercies come
    to me, that I may live;

Because thy holy laws to me
   sweet delectation give.

[78]Lord, let the proud ashamed be;
   for they, without a cause,
With me perversely dealt: but I
   will muse upon thy laws.

[79]Let such as fear thee, and have known
   thy statutes, turn to me.
[80]My heart let in thy laws be sound,
   that shamed I never be.

Psalm 119
Caph, The 11th Part

8,6,8,6

[81]My soul for thy salvation faints;
   yet I thy word believe.
[82]Mine eyes fail for thy word: I say,
   When wilt thou comfort give?

[83]For like a bottle I'm become,
   that in the smoke is set:
I'm black, and parched with grief; yet I
   thy statutes not forget.

[84]How many are thy servant's days?
   when wilt thou execute
Just judgment on these wicked men
   that do me persecute?

[85]The proud have digged pits for me,
   which is against thy laws.
[86]Thy words all faithful are: help me,
   pursued without a cause.

[87]They so consumed me, that on earth
   my life they scarce did leave:
Thy precepts yet forsook I not,
   but close to them did cleave.

⁸⁸After thy loving-kindness, Lord,
    me quicken, and preserve:
The testimony of thy mouth
    so shall I still observe.

Psalm 119
Lamed, The 12th Part

8,6,8,6

⁸⁹Thy word for ever is, O Lord,
    in heaven settled fast;
⁹⁰Unto all generations
    thy faithfulness doth last:

The earth thou hast established,
    and it abides by thee.
⁹¹This day they stand as thou ordain'dst;
    for all thy servants be.

⁹²Unless in thy most perfect law
    my soul delights had found,
I should have perished, when as
    my troubles did abound.

⁹³Thy precepts I will ne'er forget;
    they quick'ning to me brought.
⁹⁴Lord, I am thine; O save thou me:
    thy precepts I have sought.

⁹⁵For me the wicked have laid wait,
    me seeking to destroy:
But I thy testimonies true
    consider will with joy.

⁹⁶An end of all perfection
    here have I seen, O God:
But as for thy commandement,
    it is exceeding broad.

Psalm 119
Mem, The 13th Part

8,6,8,6

[97]O how love I thy law! it is
   my study all the day:
[98]It makes me wiser than my foes;
   for it doth with me stay.

[99]Than all my teachers now I have
   more understanding far;
Because my meditation
   thy testimonies are.

[100]In understanding I excel
   those that are ancients;
For I endeavoured to keep
   all thy commandements.

[101]My feet from each ill way I stayed,
   that I may keep thy word.
[102]I from thy judgments have not swerved;
   for thou hast taught me, Lord.

[103]How sweet unto my taste, O Lord,
   are all thy words of truth!
Yea, I do find them sweeter far
   than honey to my mouth.

[104]I through thy precepts, that are pure,
   do understanding get;
I therefore ev'ry way that's false
   with all my heart do hate.

Psalm 119
Nun, The 14th Part

8,6,8,6

[105]Thy word is to my feet a lamp,
   and to my path a light.
[106]I sworn have, and I will perform,
   to keep thy judgments right.

[107]I am with sore affliction
   ev'n overwhelmed, O Lord:

In mercy raise and quicken me,
   according to thy word.

108The free-will off'rings of my mouth
   accept, I thee beseech:
And unto me thy servant, Lord,
   thy judgments clearly teach.

109Though still my soul be in my hand,
   thy laws I'll not forget.
110I erred not from them, though for me
   the wicked snares did set.

111I of thy testimonies have
   above all things made choice,
To be my heritage for aye;
   for they my heart rejoice.

112I carefully inclined have
   my heart still to attend;
That I thy statutes may perform
   alway unto the end.

Psalm 119
Samech, The 15th Part

8,6,8,6

113I hate the thoughts of vanity,
   but love thy law do I.
114My shield and hiding-place thou art:
   I on thy word rely.

115All ye that evil-doers are
   from me depart away;
For the commandments of my God
   I purpose to obey.

116According to thy faithful word
   uphold and stablish me,
That I may live, and of my hope
   ashamed never be.

117Hold thou me up, so shall I be
   in peace and safety still;

And to thy statutes have respect
   continually I will.

[118]Thou tread'st down all that love to stray;
   false their deceit doth prove.
[119]Lewd men, like dross, away thou putt'st;
   therefore thy law I love.

[120]For fear of thee my very flesh
   doth tremble, all dismayed;
And of thy righteous judgments, Lord,
   my soul is much afraid.

Psalm 119
Ain, The 16th Part

8,6,8,6

[121]To all men I have judgment done,
   performing justice right;
Then let me not be left unto
   my fierce oppressors' might.

[122]For good unto thy servant, Lord,
   thy servant's surety be:
From the oppression of the proud
   do thou deliver me.

[123]Mine eyes do fail with looking long
   for thy salvation,
The word of thy pure righteousness
   while I do wait upon.

[124]In mercy with thy servant deal,
   thy laws me teach and show.
[125]I am thy servant, wisdom give,
   that I thy laws may know.

[126]'Tis time thou work, Lord; for they have
   made void thy law divine.
[127]Therefore thy precepts more I love
   than gold, yea, gold most fine.

¹²⁸Concerning all things thy commands
 all right I judge therefore;
And ev'ry false and wicked way
 I perfectly abhor.

Psalm 119
Pe, The 17th Part

8,6,8,6

¹²⁹Thy statutes, Lord, are wonderful,
 my soul them keeps with care.
¹³⁰The entrance of thy words gives light,
 makes wise who simple are.

¹³¹My mouth I have wide opened,
 and panted earnestly,
While after thy commandements
 I longed exceedingly.

¹³²Look on me, Lord, and merciful
 do thou unto me prove,
As thou art wont to do to those
 thy name who truly love.

¹³³O let my footsteps in thy word
 aright still ordered be:
Let no iniquity obtain
 dominion over me.

¹³⁴From man's oppression save thou me;
 so keep thy laws I will.
¹³⁵Thy face make on thy servant shine;
 teach me thy statutes still.

¹³⁶Rivers of waters from mine eyes
 did run down, when I saw
How wicked men run on in sin,
 and do not keep thy law.

Psalm 119
Tzaddi, The 18th Part

8,6,8,6

¹³⁷O Lord, thou art most righteous;
    thy judgments are upright.
¹³⁸Thy testimonies thou command'st
    most faithful are and right.

¹³⁹My zeal hath ev'n consumed me,
    because mine enemies
Thy holy words forgotten have,
    and do thy laws despise.

¹⁴⁰Thy word's most pure, therefore on it
    thy servant's love is set.
¹⁴¹Small, and despised I am, yet I
    thy precepts not forget.

¹⁴²Thy righteousness is righteousness
    which ever doth endure:
Thy holy law, Lord, also is
    the very truth most pure.

¹⁴³Trouble and anguish have me found,
    and taken hold on me:
Yet in my trouble my delight
    thy just commandments be.

¹⁴⁴Eternal righteousness is in
    thy testimonies all:
Lord, to me understanding give,
    and ever live I shall.

Psalm 119
Koph, The 19th Part

8,6,8,6

¹⁴⁵With my whole heart I cried, Lord, hear;
    I will thy word obey.
¹⁴⁶I cried to thee; save me, and I
    will keep thy laws alway.

¹⁴⁷I of the morning did prevent
    the dawning, and did cry:

> For all mine expectation
>   did on thy word rely.

> [148]Mine eyes did timeously prevent
>   the watches of the night,
> That in thy word with careful mind
>   then meditate I might.

> [149]After thy loving-kindness hear
>   my voice, that calls on thee:
> According to thy judgment, Lord,
>   revive and quicken me.

> [150]Who follow mischief they draw nigh;
>   they from thy law are far:
> [151]But thou art near, Lord; most firm truth
>   all thy commandments are.

> [152]As for thy testimonies all,
>   of old this have I tried,
> That thou hast surely founded them
>   for ever to abide.

Psalm 119
Resh, The 20th Part

8,6,8,6

> [153]Consider mine affliction,
>   in safety do me set:
> Deliver me, O Lord, for I
>   thy law do not forget.

> [154]After thy word revive thou me:
>   save me, and plead my cause.
> [155]Salvation is from sinners far;
>   for they seek not thy laws.

> [156]O Lord, both great and manifold
>   thy tender mercies be:
> According to thy judgments just,
>   revive and quicken me.

> [157]My persecutors many are,
>   and foes that do combine;

Yet from thy testimonies pure
  my heart doth not decline.

158I saw transgressors, and was grieved;
  for they keep not thy word.
159See how I love thy law! as thou
  art kind, me quicken, Lord.

160From the beginning all thy word
  hath been most true and sure:
Thy righteous judgments ev'ry one
  for evermore endure.

Psalm 119
Schin, The 21st Part

8,6,8,6

161Princes have persecuted me,
  although no cause they saw:
But still of thy most holy word
  my heart doth stand in awe.

162I at thy word rejoice, as one
  of spoil that finds great store.
163Thy law I love; but lying all
  I hate and do abhor.

164Sev'n times a-day it is my care
  to give due praise to thee;
Because of all thy judgments, Lord,
  which righteous ever be.

165Great peace have they who love thy law;
  offence they shall have none.
166I hoped for thy salvation, Lord,
  and thy commands have done.

167My soul thy testimonies pure
  observed carefully;
On them my heart is set, and them
  I love exceedingly.

168Thy testimonies and thy laws
   I kept with special care;
For all my works and ways each one
   before thee open are.

Psalm 119
Tau, The 22nd Part

8,6,8,6

169O let my earnest pray'r and cry
   come near before thee, Lord:
Give understanding unto me,
   according to thy word.

170Let my request before thee come:
   after thy word me free.
171My lips shall utter praise, when thou
   hast taught thy laws to me.

172My tongue of thy most blessed word
   shall speak, and it confess;
Because all thy commandements
   are perfect righteousness.

173Let thy strong hand make help to me:
   thy precepts are my choice.
174I longed for thy salvation, Lord,
   and in thy law rejoice.

175O let my soul live, and it shall
   give praises unto thee;
And let thy judgments gracious
   be helpful unto me.

176I, like a lost sheep, went astray;
   thy servant seek, and find:
For thy commands I suffered not
   to slip out of my mind.

Psalm 120

A Song of degrees.

8,6,8,6

¹In my distress to God I cried,
   and he gave ear to me.
²From lying lips, and guileful tongue,
   O Lord, my soul set free.

³What shall be giv'n thee? or what shall
   be done to thee, false tongue?
⁴Ev'n burning coals of juniper,
   sharp arrows of the strong.

⁵Woe's me that I in Mesech am
   a sojourner so long;
That I in tabernacles dwell
   to Kedar that belong.

⁶My soul with him that hateth peace
   hath long a dweller been.
⁷I am for peace; but when I speak,
   for battle they are keen.

Psalm 121

A Song of degrees.

8,6,8,6

¹I to the hills will lift mine eyes,
   from whence doth come mine aid.
²My safety cometh from the Lord,
   who heav'n and earth hath made.

³Thy foot he'll not let slide, nor will
   he slumber that thee keeps.
⁴Behold, he that keeps Israel,
   he slumbers not, nor sleeps.

⁵The Lord thee keeps, the Lord thy shade
   on thy right hand doth stay:
⁶The moon by night thee shall not smite,
   nor yet the sun by day.

⁷The Lord shall keep thy soul; he shall
    preserve thee from all ill.
⁸Henceforth thy going out and in
    God keep for ever will.

Psalm 122

A Song of degrees of David.

8,6,8,6

¹I joyed when to the house of God,
    Go up, they said to me.
²Jerusalem, within thy gates
    our feet shall standing be.

³Jerus'lem, as a city, is
    compactly built together:
⁴Unto that place the tribes go up,
    the tribes of God go thither:

To Isr'el's testimony, there
    to God's name thanks to pay.
⁵For thrones of judgment, ev'n the thrones
    of David's house, there stay.

⁶Pray that Jerusalem may have
    peace and felicity:
Let them that love thee and thy peace
    have still prosperity.

⁷Therefore I wish that peace may still
    within thy walls remain,
And ever may thy palaces
    prosperity retain.

⁸Now, for my friends' and brethren's sakes,
    Peace be in thee, I'll say.
⁹And for the house of God our Lord,
    I'll seek thy good alway.

Psalm 123

A Song of degrees.

8,6,8,6

¹O thou that dwellest in the heav'ns,
   I lift mine eyes to thee.
²Behold, as servants' eyes do look
   their masters' hand to see,

As handmaid's eyes her mistress' hand;
   so do our eyes attend
Upon the Lord our God, until
   to us he mercy send.

³O Lord, be gracious to us,
   unto us gracious be;
Because replenished with contempt
   exceedingly are we.

⁴Our soul is filled with scorn of those
   that at their ease abide,
And with the insolent contempt
   of those that swell in pride.

Psalm 124

A Song of degrees of David.

First Version (C.M.)
8,6,8,6

¹Had not the Lord been on our side,
   may Israel now say;
²Had not the Lord been on our side,
   when men rose us to slay;

³They had us swallowed quick, when as
   their wrath 'gainst us did flame:
⁴Waters had covered us, our soul
   had sunk beneath the stream.

⁵Then had the waters, swelling high,
   over our soul made way.
⁶Blessed be the Lord, who to their teeth
   us gave not for a prey.

⁷Our soul's escaped, as a bird
   out of the fowler's snare;
The snare asunder broken is,
   and we escaped are.

⁸Our sure and all-sufficient help
   is in Jehovah's name;
His name who did the heav'n create,
   and who the earth did frame.

Psalm 124

Second Version
10,10,10,10,10

¹Now Israel may say, and that truly,
If that the Lord had not our cause maintained;
²If that the Lord had not our right sustained,
When cruel men against us furiously
   Rose up in wrath, to make of us their prey;

³Then certainly they had devoured us all,
And swallowed quick, for ought that we could deem;
Such was their rage, as we might well esteem.
⁴And as fierce floods before them all things drown,
   So had they brought our soul to death quite down.

⁵The raging streams, with their proud swelling waves,
Had then our soul o'erwhelmed in the deep.
⁶But blessed be God, who doth us safely keep,
And hath not giv'n us for a living prey
   Unto their teeth, and bloody cruelty.

⁷Ev'n as a bird out of the fowler's snare
Escapes away, so is our soul set free:
Broke are their nets, and thus escaped we.
⁸Therefore our help is in the Lord's great name,
   Who heav'n and earth by his great pow'r did frame.

Psalm 125

A Song of degrees.

8,6,8,6

¹They in the Lord that firmly trust
  shall be like Zion hill,
Which at no time can be removed,
  but standeth ever still.

²As round about Jerusalem
  the mountains stand alway,
The Lord his folk doth compass so,
  from henceforth and for aye.

³For ill men's rod upon the lot
  of just men shall not lie;
Lest righteous men stretch forth their hands
  unto iniquity.

⁴Do thou to all those that be good
  thy goodness, Lord, impart;
And do thou good to those that are
  upright within their heart.

⁵But as for such as turn aside
  after their crooked way,
God shall lead forth with wicked men:
  on Isr'el peace shall stay.

Psalm 126

A Song of degrees.

8,6,8,6

¹When Zion's bondage God turned back,
    as men that dreamed were we.
²Then filled with laughter was our mouth,
    our tongue with melody:

They 'mong the heathen said, The Lord
    great things for them hath wrought.
³The Lord hath done great things for us,
    whence joy to us is brought.

⁴As streams of water in the south,
    our bondage, Lord, recall.
⁵Who sow in tears, a reaping time
    of joy enjoy they shall.

⁶That man who, bearing precious seed,
    in going forth doth mourn,
He doubtless, bringing back his sheaves,
    rejoicing shall return.

Psalm 127

A Song of degrees for Solomon.

8,6,8,6

¹Except the Lord do build the house,
    the builders lose their pain:
Except the Lord the city keep,
    the watchmen watch in vain.

²'Tis vain for you to rise betimes,
    or late from rest to keep,
To feed on sorrows' bread; so gives
    he his beloved sleep.

³Lo, children are God's heritage,
    the womb's fruit his reward.
⁴The sons of youth as arrows are,
    for strong men's hands prepared.

⁵O happy is the man that hath
   his quiver filled with those;
They unashamed in the gate
   shall speak unto their foes.

Psalm 128

A Song of degrees.

8,6,8,6

¹Blessed is each one that fears the Lord,
   and walketh in his ways;
²For of thy labour thou shalt eat,
   and happy be always.

³Thy wife shall as a fruitful vine
   by thy house' sides be found:
Thy children like to olive-plants
   about thy table round.

⁴Behold, the man that fears the Lord,
   thus blessed shall he be.
⁵The Lord shall out of Zion give
   his blessing unto thee:

Thou shalt Jerus'lem's good behold
   whilst thou on earth dost dwell.
⁶Thou shalt thy children's children see,
   and peace on Israel.

Psalm 129

A Song of degrees.

8,6,8,6

¹Oft did they vex me from my youth,
   may Isr'el now declare;
²Oft did they vex me from my youth,
   yet not victorious were.

³The plowers plowed upon my back;
   they long their furrows drew.
⁴The righteous Lord did cut the cords
   of the ungodly crew.

⁵Let Zion's haters all be turned
   back with confusion.

⁶As grass on houses' tops be they,
    which fades ere it be grown:

⁷Whereof enough to fill his hand
    the mower cannot find;
Nor can the man his bosom fill,
    whose work is sheaves to bind.

⁸Neither say they who do go by,
    God's blessing on you rest:
We in the name of God the Lord
    do wish you to be blessed.

Psalm 130

A Song of degrees.

8,6,8,6

¹Lord, from the depths to thee I cried.
    ²My voice, Lord, do thou hear:
Unto my supplication's voice
    give an attentive ear.

³Lord, who shall stand, if thou, O Lord,
    should'st mark iniquity?
⁴But yet with thee forgiveness is,
    that feared thou mayest be.

⁵I wait for God, my soul doth wait,
    my hope is in his word.
⁶More than they that for morning watch,
    my soul waits for the Lord;

I say, more than they that do watch
    the morning light to see.
⁷Let Israel hope in the Lord,
    for with him mercies be;

And plenteous redemption
    is ever found with him.
⁸And from all his iniquities
    he Isr'el shall redeem.

Psalm 131

A Song of degrees of David.

8,6,8,6

[1]My heart not haughty is, O Lord,
   mine eyes not lofty be;
Nor do I deal in matters great,
   or things too high for me.

[2]I surely have myself behaved
   with quiet sp'rit and mild,
As child of mother weaned: my soul
   is like a weaned child.

[3]Upon the Lord let all the hope
   of Israel rely,
Ev'n from the time that present is
   unto eternity.

Psalm 132

A Song of degrees.

8,6,8,6

[1]David, and his afflictions all,
   Lord, do thou think upon;
[2]How unto God he sware, and vowed
   to Jacob's mighty One.

[3]I will not come within my house,
   nor rest in bed at all;
[4]Nor shall mine eyes take any sleep,
   nor eyelids slumber shall;

[5]Till for the Lord a place I find,
   where he may make abode;
A place of habitation
   for Jacob's mighty God.

[6]Lo, at the place of Ephratah
   of it we understood;
And we did find it in the fields,
   and city of the wood.

[7]We'll go into his tabernacles,
   and at his footstool bow.

⁸Arise, O Lord, into thy rest,
   th' ark of thy strength, and thou.

⁹O let thy priests be clothed, Lord,
   with truth and righteousness;
And let all those that are thy saints
   shout loud for joyfulness.

¹⁰For thine own servant David's sake,
   do not deny thy grace;
Nor of thine own anointed one
   turn thou away the face.

¹¹The Lord in truth to David sware,
   he will not turn from it,
I of thy body's fruit will make
   upon thy throne to sit.

¹²My cov'nant if thy sons will keep,
   and laws to them made known,
Their children then shall also sit
   for ever on thy throne.

¹³For God of Zion hath made choice;
   there he desires to dwell.
¹⁴This is my rest, here still I'll stay;
   for I do like it well.

¹⁵Her food I'll greatly bless; her poor
   with bread will satisfy.
¹⁶Her priests I'll clothe with health; her saints
   shall shout forth joyfully.

¹⁷And there will I make David's horn
   to bud forth pleasantly:
For him that mine anointed is
   a lamp ordained have I.

¹⁸As with a garment I will clothe
   with shame his en'mies all:
But yet the crown that he doth wear
   upon him flourish shall.

Psalm 133

A Song of degrees of David.

8,6,8,6

¹Behold, how good a thing it is,
  and how becoming well,
Together such as brethren are
  in unity to dwell!

²Like precious ointment on the head,
  that down the beard did flow,
Ev'n Aaron's beard, and to the skirts,
  did of his garments go.

³As Hermon's dew, the dew that doth
  on Zion' hills descend:
For there the blessing God commands,
  life that shall never end.

Psalm 134

A Song of degrees.

8,6,8,6

¹Behold, bless ye the Lord, all ye
  that his attendants are,
Ev'n you that in God's temple be,
  and praise him nightly there.

²Your hands within God's holy place
  lift up, and praise his name.
³From Zion' hill the Lord thee bless,
  that heav'n and earth did frame.

Psalm 135

8,6,8,6

¹Praise ye the Lord, the Lord's name praise;
  his servants, praise ye God.
²Who stand in God's house, in the courts
  of our God make abode.

³Praise ye the Lord, for he is good;
  unto him praises sing:
Sing praises to his name, because
  it is a pleasant thing.

⁴For Jacob to himself the Lord
    did choose of his good pleasure,
And he hath chosen Israel
    for his peculiar treasure.

⁵Because I know assuredly
    the Lord is very great,
And that our Lord above all gods
    in glory hath his seat.

⁶What things soever pleased the Lord,
    that in the heav'n did he,
And in the earth, the seas, and all
    the places deep that be.

⁷He from the ends of earth doth make
    the vapours to ascend;
With rain he lightnings makes, and wind
    doth from his treasures send.

⁸Egypt's first-born, from man to beast
    ⁹who smote. Strange tokens he
On Phar'oh and his servants sent,
    Egypt, in midst of thee.

¹⁰He smote great nations, slew great kings:
    ¹¹Sihon of Heshbon king,
And Og of Bashan, and to nought
    did Canaan's kingdoms bring:

¹²And for a wealthy heritage
    their pleasant land he gave,
An heritage which Israel,
    his chosen folk, should have.

¹³Thy name, O Lord, shall still endure,
    and thy memorial
With honour shall continued be
    to generations all.

¹⁴For why? the righteous God will judge
    his people righteously;
Concerning those that do him serve,
    himself repent will he.

¹⁵The idols of the nations
  of silver are and gold,
And by the hands of men is made
  their fashion and mould.

¹⁶Mouths have they, but they do not speak;
  eyes, but they do not see;
¹⁷Ears have they, but hear not; and in
  their mouths no breathing be.

¹⁸Their makers are like them; so are
  all that on them rely.
¹⁹O Isr'el's house, bless God; bless God,
  O Aaron's family.

²⁰O bless the Lord, of Levi's house
  ye who his servants are;
And bless the holy name of God,
  all ye the Lord that fear.

²¹And blessed be the Lord our God
  from Zion's holy hill,
Who dwelleth at Jerusalem.
  The Lord O praise ye still.

Psalm 136

First Version
8,7,8,7

¹Give thanks to God, for good is he:
  for mercy hath he ever.
²Thanks to the God of gods give ye:
  for his grace faileth never.

³Thanks give the Lord of lords unto:
  for mercy hath he ever.
⁴Who only wonders great can do:
  for his grace faileth never.

⁵Who by his wisdom made heav'ns high:
  for mercy hath he ever.
⁶Who stretched the earth above the sea:
  for his grace faileth never.

⁷To him that made the great lights shine:
  for mercy hath he ever.

⁸The sun to rule till day decline:
   for his grace faileth never.

⁹The moon and stars to rule by night:
   for mercy hath he ever.
¹⁰Who Egypt's first-born killed outright:
   for his grace faileth never.

¹¹And Isr'el brought from Egypt land:
   for mercy hath he ever.
¹²With stretched-out arm, and with strong hand:
   for his grace faileth never.

¹³By whom the Red sea parted was:
   for mercy hath he ever.
¹⁴And through its midst made Isr'el pass:
   for his grace faileth never.

¹⁵But Phar'oh and his host did drown:
   for mercy hath he ever.
¹⁶Who through the desert led his own:
   for his grace faileth never.

¹⁷To him great kings who overthrew:
   for he hath mercy ever.
¹⁸Yea, famous kings in battle slew:
   for his grace faileth never.

¹⁹Ev'n Sihon king of Amorites:
   for he hath mercy ever.
²⁰And Og the king of Bashanites:
   for his grace faileth never.

²¹Their land in heritage to have:
   (for mercy hath he ever.)
²²His servant Isr'el right he gave:
   for his grace faileth never.

²³In our low state who on us thought:
   for he hath mercy ever.
²⁴And from our foes our freedom wrought:
   for his grace faileth never.

²⁵Who doth all flesh with food relieve:
    for he hath mercy ever.
²⁶Thanks to the God of heaven give:
    for his grace faileth never.

Psalm 136

Second Version
6,6,6,6,8,8

¹Praise God, for he is kind:
His mercy lasts for aye.
²Give thanks with heart and mind
To God of gods alway:
    For certainly
    His mercies dure
    Most firm and sure
    Eternally.

³The Lord of lords praise ye,
Whose mercies still endure.
⁴Great wonders only he
Doth work by his great pow'r
    For certainly
    His mercies dure
    Most firm and sure
    Eternally.

⁵Which God omnipotent,
By might and wisdom high,
The heav'n and firmament
Did frame, as we may see:
    For certainly
    His mercies dure
    Most firm and sure
    Eternally.

⁶To him who did outstretch
This earth so great and wide,
Above the waters' reach
Making it to abide:
    For certainly
    His mercies dure
    Most firm and sure
    Eternally.

7Great lights he made to be;
For his grace lasteth aye:
8Such as the sun we see,
To rule the lightsome day:
    For certainly
    His mercies dure
    Most firm and sure
    Eternally.

9Also the moon so clear,
Which shineth in our sight;
The stars that do appear,
To guide the darksome night:
    For certainly
    His mercies dure
    Most firm and sure
    Eternally.

10To him that Egypt smote,
Who did his message scorn;
And in his anger hot
Did kill all their first-born:
    For certainly
    His mercies dure
    Most firm and sure
    Eternally.

11Thence Isr'el out he brought;
For his grace lasteth ever.
12With a strong hand he wrought,
And stretched-out arm deliver:
    For certainly
    His mercies dure
    Most firm and sure
    Eternally.

13The sea he cut in two;
For his grace lasteth still.
14And through its midst to go
Made his own Israel:
    For certainly
    His mercies dure
    Most firm and sure
    Eternally.

¹⁵But overwhelmed and lost
Was proud king Pharaoh,
With all his mighty host,
And chariots there also:
    For certainly
    His mercies dure
    Most firm and sure
    Eternally.

¹⁶To him who pow'rfully
His chosen people led,
Ev'n through the desert dry,
And in that place them fed:
    For certainly
    His mercies dure
    Most firm and sure
    Eternally.

¹⁷To him great kings who smote;
For his grace hath no bound.
¹⁸Who slew, and spared not
Kings famous and renowned:
    For certainly
    His mercies dure
    Most firm and sure
    Eternally.

¹⁹Sihon the Am'rites' king;
For his grace lasteth ever:
²⁰Og also, who did reign
The land of Bashan over:
    For certainly
    His mercies dure
    Most firm and sure
    Eternally.

²¹Their land by lot he gave;
For his grace faileth never,
²²That Isr'el might it have
In heritage for ever:
    For certainly
    His mercies dure
    Most firm and sure
    Eternally.

²³Who hath remembered
Us in our low estate;
²⁴And us delivered
From foes which did us hate:
 For certainly
 His mercies dure
 Most firm and sure
 Eternally.

²⁵Who to all flesh gives food;
For his grace faileth never.
²⁶Give thanks to God most good,
The God of heav'n, for ever:
 For certainly
 His mercies dure
 Most firm and sure
 Eternally.

Psalm 137

8,6,8,6

¹By Babel's streams we sat and wept,
 when Zion we thought on.
²In midst thereof we hanged our harps
 the willow-trees upon.

³For there a song required they,
 who did us captive bring:
Our spoilers called for mirth, and said,
 A song of Zion sing.

⁴O how the Lord's song shall we sing
 within a foreign land?
⁵If thee, Jerus'lem, I forget,
 skill part from my right hand.

⁶My tongue to my mouth's roof let cleave,
 if I do thee forget,
Jerusalem, and thee above
 my chief joy do not set.

⁷Remember Edom's children, Lord,
 who in Jerus'lems day,
Ev'n unto its foundation,
 Raze, raze it quite, did say.

⁸O daughter thou of Babylon,
   near to destruction;
Blessed shall he be that thee rewards,
   as thou to us hast done.

⁹Yea, happy surely shall he be
   thy tender little ones
Who shall lay hold upon, and them
   shall dash against the stones.

Psalm 138

A Psalm of David.

8,6,8,6

¹Thee will I praise with all my heart,
   I will sing praise to thee
²Before the gods: And worship will
   toward thy sanctuary.

I'll praise thy name, ev'n for thy truth,
   and kindness of thy love;
For thou thy word hast magnified
   all thy great name above.

³Thou didst me answer in the day
   when I to thee did cry;
And thou my fainting soul with strength
   didst strengthen inwardly.

⁴All kings upon the earth that are
   shall give thee praise, O Lord,
When as they from thy mouth shall hear
   thy true and faithful word.

⁵Yea, in the righteous ways of God
   with gladness they shall sing:
For great's the glory of the Lord;
   who doth for ever reign.

⁶Though God be high, yet he respects
   all those that lowly be;
Whereas the proud and lofty ones
   afar off knoweth he.

⁷Though I in midst of trouble walk,
    I life from thee shall have:
'Gainst my foes' wrath thou'lt stretch thine hand;
    thy right hand shall me save.

⁸Surely that which concerneth me
    the Lord will perfect make:
Lord, still thy mercy lasts; do not
    thine own hands' works forsake.

Psalm 139

To the chief Musician, A Psalm of David.

8,6,8,6

¹O Lord, thou hast me searched and known.
    ²Thou know'st my sitting down,
And rising up; yea, all my thoughts
    afar to thee are known.

³My footsteps, and my lying down,
    thou compassest always;
Thou also most entirely art
    acquaint with all my ways.

⁴For in my tongue, before I speak,
    not any word can be,
But altogether, lo, O Lord,
    it is well known to thee.

⁵Behind, before, thou hast beset,
    and laid on me thine hand.
⁶Such knowledge is too strange for me,
    too high to understand.

⁷From thy Sp'rit whither shall I go?
    or from thy presence fly?
⁸Ascend I heav'n, lo, thou art there;
    there, if in hell I lie.

⁹Take I the morning wings, and dwell
    in utmost parts of sea;
¹⁰Ev'n there, Lord, shall thy hand me lead,
    thy right hand hold shall me.

[11]If I do say that darkness shall
    me cover from thy sight,
Then surely shall the very night
    about me be as light.

[12]Yea, darkness hideth not from thee,
    but night doth shine as day:
To thee the darkness and the light
    are both alike alway.

[13]For thou possessed hast my reins,
    and thou hast covered me,
When I within my mother's womb
    inclosed was by thee.

[14]Thee will I praise; for fearfully
    and strangely made I am;
Thy works are marv'llous, and right well
    my soul doth know the same.

[15]My substance was not hid from thee,
    when as in secret I
Was made; and in earth's lowest parts
    was wrought most curiously.

[16]Thine eyes my substance did behold,
    yet being unperfect;
And in the volume of thy book
    my members all were writ;

Which after in continuance
    were fashioned ev'ry one,
When as they yet all shapeless were,
    and of them there was none.

[17]How precious also are thy thoughts,
    O gracious God, to me!
And in their sum how passing great
    and numberless they be!

[18]If I should count them, than the sand
    they more in number be:
What time soever I awake,
    I ever am with thee.

¹⁹Thou, Lord, wilt sure the wicked slay:
   hence from me bloody men.
²⁰Thy foes against thee loudly speak,
   and take thy name in vain.

²¹Do not I hate all those, O Lord,
   that hatred bear to thee?
With those that up against thee rise
   can I but grieved be?

²²With perfect hatred them I hate,
   my foes I them do hold.
²³Search me, O God, and know my heart,
   try me, my thoughts unfold:

²⁴And see if any wicked way
   there be at all in me;
And in thine everlasting way
   to me a leader be.

Psalm 140

To the chief Musician, A Psalm of David.

8,6,8,6

¹Lord, from the ill and froward man
   give me deliverance,
And do thou safe preserve me from
   the man of violence:

²Who in their heart mischievous things
   are meditating ever;
And they for war assembled are
   continually together.

³Much like unto a serpent's tongue
   their tongues they sharp do make;
And underneath their lips there lies
   the poison of a snake.

⁴Lord, keep me from the wicked's hands,
   from vi'lent men me save;
Who utterly to overthrow
   my goings purposed have.

⁵The proud for me a snare have hid,
    and cords; yea, they a net
Have by the way-side for me spread;
    they gins for me have set.

⁶I said unto the Lord, Thou art
    my God: unto the cry
Of all my supplications,
    Lord, do thine ear apply.

⁷O God the Lord, who art the strength
    of my salvation:
A cov'ring in the day of war
    my head thou hast put on.

⁸Unto the wicked man, O Lord,
    his wishes do not grant;
Nor further thou his ill device,
    lest they themselves should vaunt.

⁹As for the head and chief of those
    about that compass me,
Ev'n by the mischief of their lips
    let thou them covered be.

¹⁰Let burning coals upon them fall,
    them throw in fiery flame,
And in deep pits, that they no more
    may rise out of the same.

¹¹Let not an evil speaker be
    on earth established:
Mischief shall hunt the vi'lent man,
    till he be ruined.

¹²I know God will th' afflicted's cause
    maintain, and poor men's right.
¹³Surely the just shall praise thy name;
    th' upright dwell in thy sight.

Psalm 141

A Psalm of David.

8,6,8,6

¹O Lord, I unto thee do cry,
 do thou make haste to me,
And give an ear unto my voice,
 when I cry unto thee.

²As incense let my prayer be
 directed in thine eyes;
And the uplifting of my hands
 as th' ev'ning sacrifice.

³Set, Lord, a watch before my mouth,
 keep of my lips the door.
⁴My heart incline thou not unto
 the ills I should abhor,

To practise wicked works with men
 that work iniquity;
And with their delicates my taste
 let me not satisfy.

⁵Let him that righteous is me smite,
 it shall a kindness be;
Let him reprove, I shall it count
 a precious oil to me:

Such smiting shall not break my head;
 for yet the time shall fall,
When I in their calamities
 to God pray for them shall.

⁶When as their judges down shall be
 in stony places cast,
Then shall they hear my words; for they
 shall sweet be to their taste.

⁷About the grave's devouring mouth
 our bones are scattered round,
As wood which men do cut and cleave
 lies scattered on the ground.

⁸But unto thee, O God the Lord,
 mine eyes uplifted be:
My soul do not leave destitute;
 my trust is set on thee.

⁹Lord, keep me safely from the snares
 which they for me prepare;
And from the subtle gins of them
 that wicked workers are.

¹⁰Let workers of iniquity
 into their own nets fall,
Whilst I do, by thine help, escape
 the danger of them all.

Psalm 142

Maschil of David; A Prayer when he was in the cave.

8,6,8,6

¹I with my voice cried to the Lord,
 with it made my request:
²Poured out to him my plaint, to him
 my trouble I expressed.

³When in me was o'erwhelmed my sp'rit,
 then well thou knew'st my way;
Where I did walk a snare for me
 they privily did lay.

⁴I looked on my right hand, and viewed,
 but none to know me were;
All refuge failed me, no man
 did for my soul take care.

⁵I cried to thee; I said, Thou art
 my refuge, Lord, alone;
And in the land of those that live
 thou art my portion.

⁶Because I am brought very low,
 attend unto my cry:
Me from my persecutors save,
 who stronger are than I.

⁷From prison bring my soul, that I
   thy name may glorify:
The just shall compass me, when thou
   with me deal'st bounteously.

Psalm 143

A Psalm of David.

First Version (C.M.)
8,6,8,6

¹Lord, hear my pray'r, attend my suits;
   and in thy faithfulness
Give thou an answer unto me,
   and in thy righteousness.

²Thy servant also bring thou not
   in judgment to be tried:
Because no living man can be
   in thy sight justified.

³For th' en'my hath pursued my soul,
   my life to ground down tread:
In darkness he hath made me dwell,
   as who have long been dead.

⁴My sp'rit is therefore overwhelmed
   in me perplexedly;
Within me is my very heart
   amazed wondrously.

⁵I call to mind the days of old,
   to meditate I use
On all thy works; upon the deeds
   I of thy hands do muse.

⁶My hands to thee I stretch; my soul
   thirsts, as dry land, for thee.
⁷Haste, Lord, to hear, my spirit fails:
   hide not thy face from me;

Lest like to them I do become
   that go down to the dust.
⁸At morn let me thy kindness hear;
   for in thee do I trust.

Teach me the way that I should walk:
   I lift my soul to thee.
⁹Lord, free me from my foes; I flee
   to thee to cover me.

¹⁰Because thou art my God, to do
   thy will do me instruct:
Thy Sp'rit is good, me to the land
   of uprightness conduct.

¹¹Revive and quicken me, O Lord,
   ev'n for thine own name's sake;
And do thou, for thy righteousness,
   my soul from trouble take.

¹²And of thy mercy slay my foes;
   let all destroyed be
That do afflict my soul: for I
   a servant am to thee.

Psalm 143

Second Version
6,6,6,6

¹Oh, hear my prayer, Lord,
   And unto my desire
To bow thine ear accord,
   I humbly thee require;
And, in thy faithfulness,
   Unto me answer make,
And, in thy righteousness,
   Upon me pity take.

²In judgment enter not
   With me thy servant poor;
For why, this well I wot,
   No sinner can endure
The sight of thee, O God:
   If thou his deeds shalt try,
He dare make none abode
   Himself to justify.

³Behold, the cruel foe
   Me persecutes with spite,
My soul to overthrow:
   Yea, he my life down quite
Unto the ground hath smote,
   And made me dwell full low
In darkness, as forgot,
   Or men dead long ago.

⁴Therefore my sp'rit much vexed,
   O'erwhelmed is me within;
My heart right sore perplexed
   And desolate hath been.
⁵Yet I do call to mind
   What ancient days record,
Thy works of ev'ry kind
   I think upon, O Lord.

⁶Lo, I do stretch my hands
   To thee, my help alone;
For thou well understands
   All my complaint and moan:
My thirsting soul desires,
   And longeth after thee,
As thirsty ground requires
   With rain refreshed to be.

⁷Lord, let my pray'r prevail,
   To answer it make speed;
For, lo, my sp'rit doth fail:
   Hide not thy face in need;
Lest I be like to those
   That do in darkness sit,
Or him that downward goes
   Into the dreadful pit.

⁸Because I trust in thee,
   O Lord, cause me to hear
Thy loving-kindness free,
   When morning doth appear:
Cause me to know the way
   Wherein my path should be;
For why, my soul on high
   I do lift up to thee.

⁹From my fierce enemy
   In safety do me guide,
Because I flee to thee,
   Lord, that thou may'st me hide.
¹⁰My God alone art thou,
   Teach me thy righteousness:
Thy Sp'rit's good, lead me to
   The land of uprightness.

¹¹O Lord, for thy name's sake,
   Be pleased to quicken me;
And, for thy truth, forth take
   My soul from misery.
¹²And of thy grace destroy
   My foes, and put to shame
All who my soul annoy;
   For I thy servant am.

Psalm 144

A Psalm of David.

8,6,8,6

¹O blessed ever be the Lord,
   who is my strength and might,
Who doth instruct my hands to war,
   my fingers teach to fight.

²My goodness, fortress, my high tow'r,
   deliverer, and shield,
In whom I trust: who under me
   my people makes to yield.

³Lord, what is man, that thou of him
   dost so much knowledge take?
Or son of man, that thou of him
   so great account dost make?

⁴Man is like vanity; his days,
   as shadows, pass away.
⁵Lord, bow thy heav'ns, come down, touch thou
   the hills, and smoke shall they.

⁶Cast forth thy lightning, scatter them;
   thine arrows shoot, them rout.

⁷Thine hand send from above, me save;
     from great depths draw me out;

And from the hand of children strange,
     ⁸Whose mouth speaks vanity;
And their right hand is a right hand
     that works deceitfully.

⁹A new song I to thee will sing,
     Lord, on a psaltery;
I on a ten-stringed instrument
     will praises sing to thee.

¹⁰Ev'n he it is that unto kings
     salvation doth send;
Who his own servant David doth
     from hurtful sword defend.

¹¹O free me from strange children's hand,
     whose mouth speaks vanity;
And their right hand a right hand is
     that works deceitfully.

¹²That, as the plants, our sons may be
     in youth grown up that are;
Our daughters like to corner-stones,
     carved like a palace fair.

¹³That to afford all kind of store
     our garners may be filled;
That our sheep thousands, in our streets
     ten thousands they may yield.

¹⁴That strong our oxen be for work,
     that no in-breaking be,
Nor going out; and that our streets
     may from complaints be free.

¹⁵Those people blessed are who be
     in such a case as this;
Yea, blessed all those people are,
     whose God Jehovah is.

Psalm 145

David's Psalm of praise.

First Version (C.M.)
8,6,8,6

¹I'll thee extol, my God, O King;
   I'll bless thy name always.
²Thee will I bless each day, and will
   thy name for ever praise.

³Great is the Lord, much to be praised;
   his greatness search exceeds.
⁴Race unto race shall praise thy works,
   and show thy mighty deeds.

⁵I of thy glorious majesty
   the honour will record;
I'll speak of all thy mighty works,
   which wondrous are, O Lord.

⁶Men of thine acts the might shall show,
   thine acts that dreadful are;
And I, thy glory to advance,
   thy greatness will declare.

⁷The mem'ry of thy goodness great
   they largely shall express;
With songs of praise they shall extol
   thy perfect righteousness.

⁸The Lord is very gracious,
   in him compassions flow;
In mercy he is very great,
   and is to anger slow.

⁹The Lord Jehovah unto all
   his goodness doth declare;
And over all his other works
   his tender mercies are.

¹⁰Thee all thy works shall praise, O Lord,
   and thee thy saints shall bless;
¹¹They shall thy kingdom's glory show,
   thy pow'r by speech express:

^{12}To make the sons of men to know
    his acts done mightily,
And of his kingdom th' excellent
    and glorious majesty.

^{13}Thy kingdom shall for ever stand,
    thy reign through ages all.
^{14}God raiseth all that are bowed down,
    upholdeth all that fall.

^{15}The eyes of all things wait on thee,
    the giver of all good;
And thou, in time convenient,
    bestow'st on them their food:

^{16}Thine hand thou open'st lib'rally,
    and of thy bounty gives
Enough to satisfy the need
    of ev'ry thing that lives.

^{17}The Lord is just in all his ways,
    holy in his works all.
^{18}God's near to all that call on him,
    in truth that on him call.

^{19}He will accomplish the desire
    of those that do him fear:
He also will deliver them,
    and he their cry will hear.

^{20}The Lord preserves all who him love,
    that nought can them annoy:
But he all those that wicked are
    will utterly destroy.

^{21}My mouth the praises of the Lord
    to publish cease shall never:
Let all flesh bless his holy name
    for ever and for ever.

Psalm 145

Second Version (L.M.)
8,8,8,8

[1]O Lord, thou art my God and King;
Thee will I magnify and praise:
I will thee bless, and gladly sing
   Unto thy holy name always.

[2]Each day I rise I will thee bless,
And praise thy name time without end.
[3]Much to be praised, and great God is;
   His greatness none can comprehend.

[4]Race shall thy works praise unto race,
The mighty acts show done by thee.
[5]I will speak of the glorious grace,
   And honour of thy majesty;

Thy wondrous works I will record.
[6]By men the might shall be extolled
Of all thy dreadful acts, O Lord:
   And I thy greatness will unfold.

[7]They utter shall abundantly
The mem'ry of thy goodness great;
And shall sing praises cheerfully,
   Whilst they thy righteousness relate.

[8]The Lord our God is gracious,
Compassionate is he also;
In mercy he is plenteous,
   But unto wrath and anger slow.

[9]Good unto all men is the Lord:
O'er all his works his mercy is.
[10]Thy works all praise to thee afford:
   Thy saints, O Lord, thy name shall bless.

[11]The glory of thy kingdom show
Shall they, and of thy power tell;
[12]That so men's sons his deeds may know,
   His kingdom's grace that doth excel.

¹³Thy kingdom hath none end at all,
It doth through ages all remain.
¹⁴The Lord upholdeth all that fall,
 The cast-down raiseth up again.

¹⁵The eyes of all things, Lord, attend,
And on thee wait that here do live,
And thou, in season due, dost send
 Sufficient food them to relieve.

¹⁶Yea, thou thine hand dost open wide,
And ev'ry thing dost satisfy
That lives, and doth on earth abide,
 Of thy great liberality.

¹⁷The Lord is just in his ways all,
And holy in his works each one.
¹⁸He's near to all that on him call,
 Who call in truth on him alone.

¹⁹God will the just desire fulfill
Of such as do him fear and dread:
Their cry regard, and hear he will,
 And save them in the time of need.

²⁰The Lord preserves all, more and less,
That bear to him a loving heart:
But workers all of wickedness
 Destroy will he, and clean subvert.

²¹Therefore my mouth and lips I'll frame
To speak the praises of the Lord:
To magnify his holy name
 For ever let all flesh accord.

Psalm 146

8,6,8,6

¹Praise God. The Lord praise, O my soul.
 ²I'll praise God while I live;
While I have being to my God
 in songs I'll praises give.

³Trust not in princes, nor man's son,
   in whom there is no stay:
⁴His breath departs, to's earth he turns;
   that day his thoughts decay.

⁵O happy is that man and blessed,
   whom Jacob's God doth aid;
Whose hope upon the Lord doth rest,
   and on his God is stayed:

⁶Who made the earth and heavens high,
   who made the swelling deep,
And all that is within the same;
   who truth doth ever keep:

⁷Who righteous judgment executes
   for those oppressed that be,
Who to the hungry giveth food;
   God sets the pris'ners free.

⁸The Lord doth give the blind their sight,
   the bowed down doth raise:
The Lord doth dearly love all those
   that walk in upright ways.

⁹The stranger's shield, the widow's stay,
   the orphan's help, is he:
But yet by him the wicked's way
   turned upside down shall be.

¹⁰The Lord shall reign for evermore:
   thy God, O Zion, he
Reigns to all generations.
   Praise to the Lord give ye.

Psalm 147

8,6,8,6

¹Praise ye the Lord; for it is good
   praise to our God to sing:
For it is pleasant, and to praise
   it is a comely thing.

²God doth build up Jerusalem;
   and he it is alone

That the dispersed of Israel
   doth gather into one.

3Those that are broken in their heart,
   and grieved in their minds,
He healeth, and their painful wounds
   he tenderly up-binds.

4He counts the number of the stars;
   he names them ev'ry one.
5Great is our Lord, and of great pow'r;
   his wisdom search can none.

6The Lord lifts up the meek; and casts
   the wicked to the ground.
7Sing to the Lord, and give him thanks;
   on harp his praises sound;

8Who covereth the heav'n with clouds,
   who for the earth below
Prepareth rain, who maketh grass
   upon the mountains grow.

9He gives the beast his food, he feeds
   the ravens young that cry.
10His pleasure not in horses' strength,
   nor in man's legs, doth lie.

11But in all those that do him fear
   the Lord doth pleasure take;
In those that to his mercy do
   by hope themselves betake.

12The Lord praise, O Jerusalem;
   Zion, thy God confess:
13For thy gates' bars he maketh strong;
   thy sons in thee doth bless.

14He in thy borders maketh peace;
   with fine wheat filleth thee.
15He sends forth his command on earth,
   his word runs speedily.

16Hoar-frost, like ashes, scatt'reth he;
   like wool he snow doth give:

¹⁷Like morsels casteth forth his ice;
  who in its cold can live?

¹⁸He sendeth forth his mighty word,
  and melteth them again;
His wind he makes to blow, and then
  the waters flow amain.

¹⁹The doctrine of his holy word
  to Jacob he doth show;
His statutes and his judgments he
  gives Israel to know.

²⁰To any nation never he
  such favour did afford;
For they his judgments have not known.
  O do ye praise the Lord.

Psalm 148

First version (C.M.)
8,6,8,6

¹Praise God. From heavens praise the Lord,
  in heights praise to him be.
²All ye his angels, praise ye him;
  his hosts all, praise him ye.

³O praise ye him, both sun and moon,
  praise him, all stars of light.
⁴Ye heav'ns of heav'ns him praise, and floods
  above the heavens' height.

⁵Let all the creatures praise the name
  of our almighty Lord:
For he commanded, and they were
  created by his word.

⁶He also, for all times to come,
  hath them established sure;
He hath appointed them a law,
  which ever shall endure.

⁷Praise ye Jehovah from the earth,
  dragons, and ev'ry deep:

⁸Fire, hail, snow, vapour, stormy wind,
   his word that fully keep.

⁹All hills and mountains, fruitful trees,
   and all ye cedars high:
¹⁰Beasts, and all cattle, creeping things,
   and all ye birds that fly.

¹¹Kings of the earth, all nations,
   princes, earth's judges all:
¹²Both young men, yea, and maidens too,
   old men, and children small.

¹³Let them God's name praise; for his name
   alone is excellent:
His glory reacheth far above
   the earth and firmament.

¹⁴His people's horn, the praise of all
   his saints, exalteth he;
Ev'n Isr'el's seed, a people near
   to him. The Lord praise ye.

Psalm 148

Second Version
6,6,6,6,8,8

¹The Lord of heav'n confess,
On high his glory raise.
²Him let all angels bless,
Him all his armies praise.
   ³Him glorify
   Sun, moon, and stars;
   ⁴Ye higher spheres,
   And cloudy sky.

⁵From God your beings are,
Him therefore famous make;
You all created were,
When he the word but spake.
   ⁶And from that place,
   Where fixed you be
   By his decree,
   You cannot pass.

⁷Praise God from earth below,
Ye dragons, and ye deeps:
⁸Fire, hail, clouds, wind, and snow.
Whom in command he keeps.
　⁹Praise ye his name,
　Hills great and small,
　Trees low and tall;
　¹⁰Beasts wild and tame;

All things that creep or fly.
¹¹Ye kings, ye vulgar throng,
All princes mean or high;
¹²Both men and virgins young,
　Ev'n young and old,
　¹³Exalt his name;
　For much his fame
　Should be extolled.

O let God's name be praised
Above both earth and sky;
¹⁴For he his saints hath raised,
And set their horn on high;
　Ev'n those that be
　Of Isr'el's race,
　Near to his grace.
　The Lord praise ye.

Psalm 149

8,6,8,6

¹Praise ye the Lord: unto him sing
　a new song, and his praise
In the assembly of his saints
　in sweet psalms do ye raise.

²Let Isr'el in his Maker joy,
　and to him praises sing:
Let all that Zion's children are
　be joyful in their King.

³O let them unto his great name
　give praises in the dance;
Let them with timbrel and with harp
　in songs his praise advance.

⁴For God doth pleasure take in those
    that his own people be;
And he with his salvation
    the meek will beautify.

⁵And in his glory excellent
    let all his saints rejoice:
Let them to him upon their beds
    aloud lift up their voice.

⁶Let in their mouth aloft be raised
    the high praise of the Lord,
And let them have in their right hand
    a sharp two-edged sword;

⁷To execute the vengeance due
    upon the heathen all,
And make deserved punishment
    upon the people fall.

⁸And ev'n with chains, as pris'ners, bind
    their kings that them command;
Yea, and with iron fetters strong,
    the nobles of their land.

⁹On them the judgment to perform
    found written in his word:
This honour is to all his saints.
    O do ye praise the Lord.

Psalm 150

8,6,8,6

¹Praise ye the Lord. God's praise within
    his sanctuary raise;
And to him in the firmament
    of his pow'r give ye praise.

²Because of all his mighty acts,
    with praise him magnify:
O praise him, as he doth excel
    in glorious majesty.

[3]Praise him with trumpet's sound; his praise
   with psaltery advance:
[4]With timbrel, harp, stringed instruments,
   and organs, in the dance.

[5]Praise him on cymbals loud; him praise
   on cymbals sounding high.
[6]Let each thing breathing praise the Lord.
   Praise to the Lord give ye.

GLOSSARY

contemn – to scorn or despise

cony – rock-badger

froward – defiantly opposed

imbrue – to dip, soak or stain

kythe – to make known or become known

sith – since

timeously – timely

wight – being

wonted – usual

wot – know

CPSIA information can be obtained at www.ICGtesting.com
Printed in the USA
BVOW04s0745011014

369037BV00001B/174/P